High Profiles

A comedy

Woodrow Wyatt

Samuel French - London
New York - Toronto - Hollywood

HIGH PROFILES

High Profiles was first presented under the title *The Division Belle*, by Allan Davis Ltd in association with Lee Menzies and Nick Salmon at the Theatre Royal, Margate, in October 1989. The cast was as follows:

Philip Grantly MP	Bruce Montague
Victoria Grantly	Caroline Blakiston
Julian Grantly	Ian Targett
Hyacinth	Sasha York
Maud	Fanny Carby
Jack Collingwood MP	Michael Medwin
Jane Trafford	Wendy Padbury
Sir Edgar Wiseman	Richard Caldicot

Directed by Allan Davis
Designed by John Page

CHARACTERS

Philip Grantly MP
Victoria Grantly, *his wife*
Julian Grantly, *his son*
Hyacinth Grantly, *his daughter*
Maud, *his housekeeper*
Jack Collingwood, *his friend*
Jane Trafford, *his Private Secretary*
Sir Edgar Wiseman, *a solicitor*

The action takes place in a luxury flat in Westminster and the *Garrick Club*.

Time—the end of June, 1990

The set of the Margate production

ACT I

Scene 1

A man is discovered in a spotlight. He is Philip Grantly, an MP in his middle years, handsome, assured and well dressed

Philip I don't believe it's true. First thing yesterday morning was like first thing any other Friday morning. Well, almost, apart from a touch of pleasant anticipation. The Romans called Friday the day of Venus, the goddess of sensual love. Philip, I said to myself, you're a lucky fellow; not like those miserable buggers never satisfied with what they've got, always complaining that life deals them a rotten hand and no one understands how good they are. That's not my problem. I've worked hard. I've said the right things. I've got on thanks to Mrs Thatcher liking me. I enjoy what little political power I've had so far. People looking to see who's in the official car as it emerges from the Foreign Office into Whitehall. The flattering pomp on official visits abroad. The delicate deference of civil servants who are cleverer than me. Although I'm only a Minister of State at the Foreign Office and not yet in the Cabinet it's a good base for knowing all the right people in or out of politics. I was feeling pleased with myself. Nothing can stop me I thought. Perhaps that was the trouble. The Ancient Greeks said the gods didn't like it when mortals preened themselves too much. They were hit by unexpected blows on the back of the head when they thought nothing could go wrong.

Black-out

Scene 2

It is Friday morning. The sun is shining

The large sitting room of a luxury flat in Westminster. Windows in one wall look over the court and on to windows of flats in the block opposite. Folding glass doors at the back of the room when opened wide, as they are now, show the entrance hall, front door and a passage leading off to the bedrooms, etc. The room is furnished with conventional, elegant and expensive taste. In addition to a sofa which has a rug in front of it are armchairs, occasional tables, lamps, a wastepaper basket, vases and pictures etc. On one side of the room stands a dining table with four chairs around it and a small sideboard with a hot-plate. There are bottles, glasses and a small fridge, all possibly set into a cupboard

The stage is empty. The telephone is ringing as Maud enters, pushing a trolley with breakfast things on it. She is a middle-aged woman with a pleasant, worn face, wearing a neat semi-uniform overall. A cross between a cook-house-keeper and a parlour maid, she has a special position with the family so does not call Mrs Grantly "Madam" and she calls the two children by their Christian names. She comes from Nottinghamshire

Maud takes a step towards the telephone when Victoria enters. She wears a close fitting silk dressing gown, expensive and fashionable and although she has been long married, her slim figure, lithe movements and vitality suggest her sexuality is not dead

Victoria I'll get it, Maud. (*She walks to the telephone and picks it up*) Treble two-six-two-nine-seven . . . It's me, Miss Trafford. How are you? . . . Mr Grantly is still shaving. . . . A message from Number Ten? . . . We're not going to Abbey House this weekend. We'll be here if the Prime Minister wants to ring him. . . . I'll tell him. He'll be on tenterhooks. . . . I hope Mr Grantly's not working you too hard. I know how much he depends on you. . . . Goodbye, Miss Trafford.

Victoria puts the telephone down and walks over to Maud who is carrying scrambled eggs and coffee to the hot-plate at the side, putting plates, cups, cereals, marmalade, butter and sugar on the breakfast table

Maud Good morning, Mrs Grantly.
Victoria Good morning, Maud.

Maud pours coffee for her

    I hope your mother's better.
Maud I spoke to the hospital last night. Mam's still a bit badly but the hip is settling down. She won't kick her clogs.
Victoria When's she coming home?
Maud Around mid-day. I'll be in time to see her.
Victoria Will she be all right when you've gone?
Maud My brother and his wife are coming in after his work. They'll stay until she's about again. The factory's only an hour and a half away.
Victoria The journey sounds a lot on top of his work.
Maud His is an easy job. He never sweats. I'll catch an evening train back from Nottingham.
Victoria Mr Grantly spilt soup on his dinner jacket at the Speaker's house last night.
Maud He's always got his togs in a mess. Ever since he was a lad and I went to work as a housemaid for his mam at Abbey House. Never changes.
Victoria Would you take the coat to the cleaners on your way to the station. It's urgent for Tuesday's dinner with the PMs *bête noir*, Jacques Delors, the ghastly man from Brussels.
Maud Was last night's a very grand dinner?
Victoria The Speaker's apartments are. The guests weren't. Just politicians.
Maud A waste of an evening.

Victoria I sat next to the Chief Whip. He's charming (*She smiles*).

As Victoria starts to leave with her coffee Julian, aged nineteen, enters from the hall. He has hair cropped at the back, long at the front, is clever and at the ranting age

Julian Good morning, Ma.
Victoria Good morning Julian. (*She gives him a peck and pats his face*) You haven't shaved very well.
Julian You're so middle class, Ma.

Victoria exits down the hall

Maud Ey up, mi duck and don't act mardarse with your mother.
Julian And a very good morning to you too and I'm not spoilt, just realistic. (*As he walks to the hot-plate*) Scrambled eggs. Great! (*He gets some and takes a seat at the table*) Is this butter or margarine? (*As he reaches to a dish on the table*)
Maud Margarine in this house. When your father's here.

Philip enters the hall. He puts his red dispatch case with the Royal Arms in the hall. He is just starting to come in to the room with a copy of the "Daily Telegraph" in his hand

Julian Oh, Christ. What vile muck. Give me butter any day.

He doesn't see Philip, who exchanges brief greetings with Maud as she goes down the hall

Philip Good morning, Maud.
Maud Good morning, Mr Grantly.

Maud exits

Philip (*going to the hot-plate to help himself*) Eat butter and die young. It's full of dangerous saturated fats.
Julian Your government pays farmers to make butter mountains. I suppose you do it to cut down the numbers needing old age pensions.
Philip I wish you Socialists weren't so humourless. We spend millions every year researching the best food for animals, none on the best food for humans. I want everyone to live longer.
Julian By not eating sausages, bacon, meat pies, chips ... Anything the working classes like. Why pick on them?

Hyacinth enters from the hall as Julian speaks. She is Philip's daughter, a vivacious, pretty, intelligent girl of seventeen

Hyacinth Oh, not the proletariat at breakfast. (*She goes to the hot-plate for scrambled eggs and coffee*) My politics teacher belongs to the Coronary Prevention Group.
Julian So what?
Hyacinth So what is that she knows what she's talking about. She says your precious working classes should eat pheasant and caviar with lemon. Full

of unsaturated fats and lovely vitamin C. (*She puts her tongue out at Julian and sits down*)

Julian Ha! Ha! Don't be so crass. Your teachers are a bunch of Tories anyway.

Hyacinth Some of them vote Labour.

Julian There's not much difference to the way Labour's gang are going.

Philip Those hypocrites are working overtime to pretend they're as good capitalists as we are.

Julian There are still enough on the real Left to sabotage the traitors to Socialism.

Hyacinth I thought you all drowned your quarrels by hating the Prime Minister.

Julian There's plenty to hate about that evil woman. She wanted the Falklands war to pose as Boadicea.

Hyacinth Rubbish.

Julian She provoked the miners' strike to win an election by putting it down.

Philip So the poor, innocent miners had nothing to do with it?

Julian She always hated the National Health Service. She thinks people are only unemployed because they're work shy.

Hyacinth She made Britain wake up.

Julian You and Dad are besotted by that bloody woman.

Philip Calling her a bloody woman is childish. She's fighting to make everyone better off.

Julian She obscenely syphons money off the poor to give it to the rich.

Philip Who for instance?

Hyacinth I know. Those left-wing loonies who make fortunes in the theatre and on TV. The sort of clowns who meet in beautiful drawing rooms to cook up half-baked plots against the Prime Minister.

Julian They're decent, civilized people even if they're not real Socialists.

Philip You mean they're so genteel that they dislike being told they can keep more of the money they earn.

Hyacinth Their moral scruples haven't stopped them making masses of loot for themselves.

Julian They're not responsible for tax cuts for the rich.

Philip You've always loved your own sitting room at Abbey House. And your horse.

Julian Personalizing serious issues doesn't stop them being valid.

Philip Tell that to those smarmy Labour leaders with a place in London and a house in the country.

Hyacinth And Labour says if they get in you won't be allowed a second house. Unless you're a top earning Socialist and you've got one already.

Julian The PM's ruined the bloody country.

Philip I hope she goes on ruining it the same way for ever. Then we'll be as rich as the Americans and the Japanese.

Julian Only a planned Socialism can do that. (*He goes to the hot-plate*)

Philip They've rumbled that rubbish in Eastern Europe. Your old fashioned Socialism is dead, Julian.

Hyacinth Mr Gorbachev and Boris Yeltsin know that.

Julian (*sitting down*) We've got a marvellous new group of the Workers' Revolutionary Party at the Poly. We're going on a protest march this evening led by some miners.

Philip Where to?

Julian The Home Secretary's flat at Whitehall Court.

Maud enters with the butter

Hyacinth If Bernard Shaw still had a flat there he'd tell you what infantile lefties you are.

Maud Here's your bit of butter, Julian.

Julian Thanks, Maud.

Maud Bernard Shaw? Didn't he write *My Fair Lady*?

Philip And a lot more besides, unfortunately.

Maud exits

Philip What's this demo against?

Julian The refusal to prosecute the police for their foul brutality and provocation to the peaceful anti poll tax campaigners in Trafalgar Square. Everyone saw it on TV.

Philip Doesn't loyalty to friends count?

Julian Not above equality and justice.

Hyacinth Like you having a Porsche and the other Poly students going by bus and underground.

Julian Shut up, Hyacinth. I use my car to distribute political literature.

Hyacinth Wouldn't a van be better?

Philip It was a mistake sending you to Harrow. I thought it was a haven of respectability.

Julian Most of the intelligent masters have leftish friends putting out unbiased programmes on the BBC and ITV.

Philip Does the Home Secretary know what you intend?

Julian No. It's a surprise.

Philip Not now it's not. I shall certainly tell him. And he'll tell the police.

Julian But everything is confidential in a private conversation in a private house. That's the convention.

Philip It's conventional not to stab your father in the back by attacking a Cabinet minister in his own government.

Julian The demo's not against you.

Philip It's against my personal interest.

Julian It's a political issue not a personal one.

Philip There's a government reshuffle this weekend. You get yourself all over the television and the papers tonight and you could blow my chances of being in the Cabinet.

Julian That's your affair, Dad.

Philip And yours. None of us in this family can escape having high profiles.

Hyacinth How gorgeous. I feel like Madonna.

Philip High profiles mean high risks.

Julian You can't stop me expressing my opinions.

Philip I can stop your allowance.
Julian That's blackmail.
Philip Blackmail's not always wrong. It can be self defence.
Julian I'm entitled to my life.
Philip And I'm entitled to mine.

Julian half-rises to reach across the table

Victoria enters carrying her coffee cup and Philip's dinner jacket. She is still wearing her dressing gown but with shoes and stockings and presumably her underwear

Victoria Don't get up for me, Julian.
Julian (*aggressively*) I wasn't, Ma. I wanted Dad's sugar-free marmalade.
Victoria (*looking at Julian who is obviously her favourite*) Once you were so charming. Now you think it's classless to be rude.
Philip That's because his head is full of cockeyed Militant Communist rubbish. He's threatening to go on a damn silly demo tonight.
Victoria He's been trying to convert me. (*Fondly*) He says the best way to defeat your enemy is to attack their soft and stupid parts first.

Victoria sits on the sofa with the dinner jacket. She looks through the pockets and finds a pen in one and a piece of paper in another. She unfolds the piece of paper. Her face changes from sunny to cloudy. She sits motionless, reading, then puts the paper in the pocket of her dressing gown

Philip Insufferable young prig.
Victoria He'll grow out of it. It's intellectual bed-wetting.
Julian (*indignantly*) It's not, Ma. Stop treating me like a baby.
Hyacinth You are one.
Julian And we're nothing to do with Militant either, Dad. They're far too tame.
Hyacinth On to the Winter Palace, Comrades!

Julian throws down his half-eaten toast and marmalade and jumps up angrily. He moves towards the front door

Julian I'll see you tonight, if you haven't gone to bed. Or not still drinking champagne at some so-called democratic embassy.
Philip Actually it's the Soviet Embassy this evening. They give us caviar as well.
Julian They would. They're not Communists since Gorbachev.
Victoria (*to Julian as he goes by*) Give me a kiss, dear, and do something to your hair.
Julian You look as if you've had a shock, Ma.
Victoria It's nothing really.
Philip Don't forget what I said about that demo. I mean it.

Julian growls, pecks his mother's cheek as he goes by and puts his hands through his hair, making a face

Julian Your lot can't stifle the will of the people.

Julian exits

Philip What an appalling boy.
Victoria Not really. You're an old bull. He's a young one. He wants to displace you as head of the herd.
Philip He certainly has a nasty air of menace.
Victoria I find it invigorating. Though I hope I'm not an old cow yet.
Hyacinth (*flinging her arms around Victoria*) You never will be, Mummy. But if Julian won it would be incest.
Victoria Bulls and cows are not so particular about that as we are.
Hyacinth I must put my books together.

Hyacinth exits

Maud comes in and goes towards the trolley

Maud Is it all right if I clear away now, Mrs Grantly?
Victoria Yes of course. And Maud, don't forget to take this to the cleaners. (*She gives the jacket to Maud*)

Philip remains where he is as Maud starts placing plates, etc. on the trolley

Stay the night with your mother if you like, Maud.

Hyacinth returns with her satchel very full

Maud There won't be any need. I've left some supper in the fridge for the children. They'll mank about with that, without mythering me with the mess they'll make if they get their own breakfast.
Hyacinth We never make a mess, Maud. And I'm ever so tidy.

At that moment Hyacinth knocks over her satchel. A couple of books and some badly home rolled cigarettes fall on the floor

Victoria (*sharply*) What are those dreadful cigarettes, Hyacinth? They look like some sort of joint.
Hyacinth (*confused*) All my friends smoke them. They don't do any harm.
Philip They lead to hard drugs.
Hyacinth That's as old fashioned as flared jeans.
Philip And I'm an old fashioned father. I'm confiscating them. (*He gets up and grabs them, squashes them and throws them in the wastepaper basket*)
Hyacinth (*defiantly*) Now I'll have to roll some more. You're a beast, Daddy.
Victoria Don't be rude to your father. It's not pleasing.
Hyacinth (*making a face*) I'm seventeen.
Philip Old enough to know better. Promise me never to smoke them again.
Hyacinth (*seeing a chance of a diversion*) Why should I?
Philip Because you'll get yourself and all of us into trouble. You know there's a Cabinet reshuffle on.
Hyacinth (*reluctantly*) All right then.
Philip You're as selfish as Julian.
Victoria You need to get going or you'll be late for school.

Hyacinth I won't be back until six or so. There's some professor coming to give a talk on the unconscious poetry in the language of the Arugiba tribe. Only he and two other Europeans understand it.

Victoria Good heavens.

Philip And that's called education.

Maud A lot of funny things go on in that school.

Maud exits with the trolley

Hyacinth The Arugiba tribe live in the rain forests of South America. Time's stood still for them, like you, Daddy.

Hyacinth gives her father a perfunctory kiss and then her mother, and vanishes through the front door

Philip Typical of your sex. She always wants the last word.

Victoria Do you think she'll get into Oxford?

Philip Easily. She has that gift for debating points they like so much.

Victoria Good training for politics.

Philip That's why more prime ministers and cabinet ministers come from Oxford than Cambridge.

Victoria And why your Cambridge friends are dimmer.

Philip No, we're cleverer. But we have higher principles. The Russians recruited all their best agents from Cambridge.

Victoria Scarcely shows high principles.

Philip It does. Think of brilliant Cambridge men like Blunt, Burgess, Maclean, Philby.

Victoria I don't see the connection.

Philip Conventionally they were traitors. But their principles made them put what they thought best for the world above their own country. No Oxford man would do that if it put his career at risk.

Victoria That's how Julian talks. It was exciting about the PM's message. Perhaps you'll be in the Cabinet.

Philip Cambridge may not be a total bar.

Victoria You've been stagnating as a Minister of State for five years.

Philip Number Ten's concern about my whereabouts may mean they want me out fast.

Victoria (*acidly*) Yes they cut out dead wood.

Philip I always speak up in support when the PM's in trouble.

Victoria I should hope so. She made you.

Philip That doesn't stop ministers making speeches from both sides of their faces. One loyal to the Prime Minister, the other sympathetic to the malcontents.

Victoria The political version of turning the other cheek.

Philip When they go too far they're out for ever.

Victoria You're obsessed by wanting to be a Cabinet Minister.

Philip The sole reason for being in politics is power. Ask that charlatan who waves his hair and arms to impress the Tory women with his warm and caring heart. It's really an icebox of cold ambition.

Victoria Don't let him hear you think that.

Philip It doesn't matter. He's blown it. He'll never be back in the Cabinet, let alone PM.

Victoria I expect you, too, think you could be Prime Minister. What vanity.

Philip All politicians are vain. Like actors. It's an occupational disease.

Victoria (*sweetly*) Don't be touchy. My teasing doesn't mean I've stopped loving you yet. I want you to be happy.

Philip I know that. It's a great strength to me.

Victoria takes from her pocket the note she found in Philip's coat, glances at it, wondering whether to show it to him, and gives him the pen

Philip Oh, thank you.

Victoria (*as she puts the note back in her pocket*) I suppose a *News of the World* type scandal could dish your chances.

Philip What put that in your head?

Victoria Something I was reading reminded me how swiftly politicians can be destroyed.

Philip No scandal in my humdrum life.

Victoria You're sure they don't think you're over the top?

Philip Why should they?

Victoria You're over the top with me. It demonstrates declining vigour. The last time you made love to me enthusiastically was the night you became a Minister of State.

Philip You're embarrassing me.

Victoria Good. It's been pretty perfunctory for ages.

Philip (*reflectively*) That's what's biting you.

Victoria You've caught on at last.

Philip Frenzied passion in a marriage is bound to wear out. Otherwise there'd be massive unemployment among the call girls.

Victoria Some of my friends think married sex goes on getting better and better.

Philip Then they're liars or deluding themselves.

Victoria Not if it's a good marriage.

Philip Good marriages advance from marriages of bodies into marriages of minds. More soothing and much less exhausting.

Victoria Boring old Darby and Joan? That's what we've come to.

Philip (*anxiously*) I sincerely hope so.

Victoria And I'm supposed to live, all passion spent, like a nun?

Philip (*anxiously again*) Don't you?

Victoria I have so far. But what did Byron say? "A man's love is a thing apart. 'Tis a woman's whole existence".

Philip Byron also said (*He declaims sonorously*)
>   "For the sword outwears its sheath,
>   And the soul outwears the breast,
>   And the heart must pause to breathe,
>   And love itself must rest".

Victoria Your sword's certainly worn out. You must live like a monk.

Philip I've no time for anything but my work.

Victoria We'd better start a monastery.

Maud enters wearing a mackintosh and carrying a large, bulging cloth bag
Victoria gives her the coat

Maud Mrs Grantly, I've left everything in the dishwasher. I've borrowed a
few things to give my mother for lunch. I hope you don't mind.
Victoria Of course not, Maud. Philip, let's send her some flowers.

*Philip pulls out his wallet and takes out two ten pound notes which Maud turns
back to receive*

Maud Thank you very much.
Victoria Please give your mother our regards.
Maud Thank you both. Mam will be very pleased.
Victoria Be sure and tell the cleaners to make it a rush job.
Maud Dunna wittle. Goodbye for now.

She exits through the front door

Philip She's got half the fridge with her.
Victoria Don't be so stingy. (*She looks at her watch*) You'll be late at the
Ministry.
Philip No hurry. I don't have a meeting till nine forty-five. What are you
doing?
Victoria A little quick shopping first. Then to meet Mary at Wimbledon.
Philip Mary who?
Victoria Jack's wife. She's got Centre Court tickets for the men's singles
semi finals. It'll be nice to look at some virile men.
Philip (*pained*) Give it a rest. Don't forget the reception at the Russian
Embassy tonight for their new Foreign Minister. We ought to be there
soon after seven.
Victoria Whatever the state of play I'll leave in time to dress.
Philip (*picking up his dispatch box*) Whatever you wear you'll be the best
looking woman.
Victoria I'll be the best dressed. Unless Mrs Gorbachev is there.
Philip Well, goodbye. Have a nice day. (*He hugs her*) I do love you. For ever
and for always.
Victoria It doesnt always feel like it.
Philip It's never changed for me.

Philip leaves by the front door

*Victoria takes out the piece of paper and reads it again. She goes to the
telephone but doesn't pick it up. It rings and she leaps to it*

Victoria (*on the phone*) Treble two-six-two-nine-seven ... Hello, Jack.
You've missed him by a fraction. ... I was about to ring you myself ...
About Philip and me ... He's doing something beastly and silly. It could
ruin our lives. ... Listen to this then. (*She takes out the piece of paper*)
"Important Memo. Exclamation Mark. This meeting is so boring,
Doggy." ... Doggy is what she calls Philip. ... She's his sly, sexy
secretary, of course. ... "Will Sir Martin never stop?" ... Don't keep

interrupting. Sir Martin's a nice old civil servant and so he can't help being boring. ... Let me go on. "I love the way your hair curls behind your ears, Doggy" ... No, not pair of pearls—your *hair curls* behind your ears ... I don't think it's funny ... Women do have a sense of humour ... Listen to how the bitch goes on. "We must get our evening drink together, so I can show off our diamond bracelet" ... Ah, now you think it could be serious ... That would be kind of you, Jack. Lucky you've no horse running at Newmarket today. Maud's gone to Nottingham so we can talk without being interrupted ... Don't ring the bell if there's an empty milk bottle outside the door. ... No, I'm not expecting the milkman. It's just a precaution ... In case Philip suddenly pops back for something he's forgotten. He does sometimes ... Don't be an ass. She's got the bracelet already.

The Lights cross-fade to Philip

SCENE 3

Spotlight on Philip

Philip After all that niggling at me by Victoria I'm looking forward to a relaxing Friday morning at the Foreign Office. No Parliamentary Questions to prepare for. They're not proper questions. They're booby traps or a way for MPs to get their names in the local papers to show their constituents what busy bees they are. There are no questions on Fridays because the Commons has to stop by four-thirty. The handful of MPs left who didn't go home on Thursday then buzz off till Monday afternoon. That gives them plenty of time to wallow in self pity about how overworked they are and to wonder whether the public are ready yet to wear MPs voting themselves another pay rise. The Lords hardly ever sit on Fridays, the lazy sods. They don't do much when they do. Perhaps Labour's right to want to abolish the House of Lords, but the Dukes and their Duchesses do look splendid when the Queen opens Parliament. No other country can touch it. But I'd die if ever I were incarcerated in the Lords. Now Sir Martin's coming to see me. He's our Permanent Under Secretary at the Foreign Office. Calm, confident, coaxing. He's rescued many a minister from his own incompetence. But I don't let him dominate me.

The Lights cross-fade to the sitting-room

SCENE 4

Later that morning

The door bell rings several times. Victoria, carrying a handbag and now wearing the outfit of a well-dressed woman ready for shopping and Wimbledon, hurries towards the door

Victoria (*shouting*) Just coming. (*She opens the door*)

Jack is standing there. Also an MP he has the interesting, lively face of a man who enjoys life and means to enjoy it more. He is about the same age as Philip and is carrying a huge bunch of red roses

Victoria Coming, Jack. My, you are impatient.

Victoria returns with Jack

Jack I'm always impatient to see you, Victoria. And to kiss you properly.

They are still standing, and he grasps her in his arms and the roses fall to the floor. Victoria pushes him away after a short struggle to free herself

Victoria I don't want you to kiss me properly.
Jack No. Improperly would be nicer.
Victoria This is not the right time to lark about.
Jack It always is the right time. (*He picks up the roses and hands them to her*)
Victoria You don't understand. I'm terribly upset about Philip.
Jack I've brought these as a small consolation.
Victoria Jack, you're sweet in some ways. (*She puts the roses in an empty vase which she fills from a jug in the drinks cupboard*) But how am I to explain them to Philip?
Jack Don't you ever buy flowers?
Victoria Not masses of red roses. They're what admirers send.
Jack You'll think of something. Women always do—they're such expert liars.
Victoria And men never lie.
Jack It's not so easy for them. It's much harder for a husband to hide what he's up to than for a wife.
Victoria You don't have much of an opinion of me.
Jack I do—the highest. I'm entranced by everything about you. Your legs, the curve of your hips.
Victoria I can't swallow your Don Juan technique while I'm devastated over Philip falling for that bloody girl.
Jack The best pick me up is knowing someone else is hooked on you.
Victoria Philip's behaviour makes me feel dirty and degraded.
Jack He's the one who's degraded by not appreciating what a fabulous creature he's got.
Victoria He evidently doesn't think so.
Jack I shall proceed with my cure.
Victoria (*laughing and flattered*) You are an ass.
Jack Before that disrespectful interruption I was about to comment on the miraculous shape of your waist, your delicious breasts.
Victoria You've never seen them.
Jack I had a good peep the other night at the dinner at Number Ten. What a relief from looking at the dreary wives most MPs and officials have.
Victoria Not much competition.
Jack You didn't seem to be wearing a bra. You must have hoped I'd be sitting next to you.

Victoria (*slightly pleased*) Men are disgusting.
Jack Don't interrupt. I'm describing something finer than the Venus de Milo.
Victoria But I've got arms.
Jack If she had, they couldn't be as delicately feminine as yours. Nor her hands.
Victoria (*blushing*) You're being ridiculous.
Jack I'm not. You have eternal youth. It shines in your eyes, it flows in your hair, it smiles in that limpid loveliness, it laughs in that adorable mouth.
Victoria You're like a soap opera star who fancies an eighteen year old waitress. Stop.
Jack I won't. You've got the most desirable body and most beautiful face I've ever seen. You're all woman. I want to worship the whole of you with my body.
Victoria (*laughing*) Now you're being corny as well as coarse.
Jack Coarse? It's what they say in church. It's called Holy Matrimony.
Victoria There's nothing holy about you. All you want is sex. Not me as a person. Not my mind. Not very enticing.
Jack Beautiful women want to be loved for their brains; brainy women for the beauty they haven't got. I love your soul as well.
Victoria (*smiling*) Blarney. I'm not as nice as you think.
Jack You couldn't do anything mean or common.
Victoria I'd use any dirty trick against anyone who threatened my family.
Jack You're wonderfully feminine. But strong.
Victoria I'm at my weakest today. In need of protection not seduction.
Jack Your voice says you want to resist me. Your heart doesn't. It didn't on Monday when I kissed you at the dance for the Injured Jockeys' Fund.
Victoria It was the drink and the music. No more sweetie pie talk till I've had your advice. (*She sits on the sofa*) No, don't sit next to me. You'll encircle me with thousands of arms like an octopus.

Jack makes a face and sits instead on a dining chair. Victoria takes the piece of paper we have seen before from her bag and hands it to him

You've got to think seriously about this.
Jack "I love the way your hair curls behind your ears, Doggy". Where did you find it?
Victoria In Philip's suit.
Jack (*shocked*) Do you go through his clothes?
Victoria Inside pockets as well. Every sensible wife does.
Jack The poor man is under constant surveillance undressed or dressed.
Victoria Of course. And if he has a locked drawer in his writing desk I rummage for a key to fit it.
Jack My God, do you think Mary's like that?
Victoria Any woman is if she loves her husband. If she values her marriage. Or if she wants to divorce him.
Jack Terrifying!

Victoria When I stop caring about Philip I'll stop reading his letters and listening to his telephone conversations. I've spoilt several promising little flirtations before he got too serious.

Jack You still love Philip.

Victoria I've been married since I was nineteen. It's not so exciting as it was but its grown more solid and real. He's mine. He's my family. He's the home I've made.

Jack The Scarlet Secretary must be pretty.

Victoria She doesn't look too bad. She's cleverer and much younger than me.

Jack The diamond bracelet's rather disturbing.

Victoria Yes, it is.

Jack In England a Minister caught having an affair with his secretary has to marry her or resign. In France they give him the *Croix de Guerre*.

Victoria Philip would love that.

Jack I suppose he's been seeing her out of the office.

Victoria He's taken to working late at the Ministry.

Jack A bad sign.

Victoria There've been more important votes than usual in the evenings. He was late on Wednesday.

Jack is silent

Wasn't there a division?

Jack (*shaking his head*) The division bell would have woken me up in the smoking room.

Victoria You're so frivolous over politics.

Jack It was a frivolous subject. An unopposed motion about divorced curates moved by that tiresome Archbishop of Canterbury.

Victoria Do you tell Mary you have to be late in the House when you're seeing someone you shouldn't?

Jack (*slowly*) We-e-ll. Most MPs would. It's what makes it such a marvellous club.

Victoria Women are attracted by power. They don't realize that MPs haven't got any.

Jack You're putting me in my place.

Victoria Nor have most Ministers. You'd think high fliers like Private Secretaries to Ministers would know that.

Jack (*glumly*) Mary picks my secretaries. She says she doesn't want another woman in her life.

Victoria Good for her. Before Philip was a Minister I vetted his—severe, elderly ladies with horn-rimmed spectacles who do their own hair.

Jack I'm sorry for Philip.

Victoria The Civil Service won't let me interfere. And they won't go back to having all males in the Private Office. Sir Martin says they'd be accused of sexism.

Jack They'd be taken before the Equal Opportunities Commission. A government body run by women to protect women's rights.

Victoria Not wives' rights. They're threatened by working women with a government approved licence to steal their husbands. Jack, you must help me stop it.

Jack He's my best friend. He'd be furious if he thought I was trying to stop his—er—fun.

Victoria Fun? She calls him "doggy". It's dementia in the kennels.

Jack No, it's human nature.

Victoria He's given her a diamond bracelet. He's never given me one.

Jack He's given you a lot of other things.

Victoria I thought you'd be on my side.

Jack I am. But we have to think it out rationally.

Victoria What do you suggest?

Jack Confront him with it. Tell him you'll make a public scandal. Bang would go his chances in the Cabinet reshuffle.

Victoria He'd mind that more than anything. How could I be so disloyal?

Jack (*moving to sit by her side on the sofa, and putting his arm around her*) You could warn him it might get into the newspapers. If they go out together often some gossip columnist is bound to notice.

Victoria (*she has not moved his arm away*) That would be such a public humiliation. It always is for the wives. (*She bursts into tears*)

Jack What are you going to do about it?

Victoria It's such a shock. I must think hard over the weekend.

Jack Will you face him with it?

Victoria Not until I'm clearer what to do.

Jack Don't hesitate to consult me.

Victoria (*putting her head on his shoulder*) I can trust you, can't I?

Jack Absolutely. I'm not unreliable like other men.

Victoria All unreliable men say that.

Jack I long to give you some of the love you deserve.

Victoria Dear Jack. I've never been unfaithful.

Jack Philip is.

Victoria That note isn't proof.

Jack Men don't give diamond bracelets just for holding hands.

Victoria I suppose not.

Jack But I'd give you one even if you never let me touch you.

Victoria That's a good line. Perhaps it's Philip's too.

Jack Don't be so disbelieving. I'd be as proud as a peacock to see you wearing something I'd given you.

Victoria Would you?

Jack You must know something you'd like.

Victoria There is but I'm not going to tell you.

Jack It's too late to be coy. Is it a diamond bracelet?

Victoria I'm afraid it is.

Jack I thought it must be in the circumstances.

Victoria You're laughing at me.

Jack No, with you. Where is it?

Victoria *Cartier*. A beautiful one I saw two weeks ago.

Jack Please buy it.

Victoria Jack, I couldn't. It wouldn't be right. Anyway it costs too much.

Jack You're making me more determined.

Victoria I wouldn't accept something so extravagant from you.

Jack Don't worry. I'm much richer than Philip.

Victoria But it'd be a colossal present.

Jack Oh, a bracelet's bound to cost much less than the filly I'm hoping to buy tonight. That'll be a quarter of a million.

Victoria Not very gallant to compare me with a horse.

Jack She's very graceful. She moves beautifully.

Victoria With an elegant compliment like that, you bowl me over.

Jack Tell them to send the bill to me.

Victoria Mary might open it.

Jack Tell them to mark it "Strictly Personal" to the House of Commons, to be opened only by me. They know me well. They've done it before.

Victoria Oh!

Jack (*quickly*) When I've bought a surprise present for Mary.

Victoria What will Philip say when he sees it?

Jack What will Mary say if she sees it?

Victoria If I think hard enough I expect I'll come up with something. Not a lie of course.

Jack (*smiling*) Of course not.

Victoria Are the jewellers discreet?

Jack It's a jeweller's business to be discreet. Like a florist.

Victoria I see why scarlet women enjoy being scarlet. It's a splendid sensation. Every woman should have it at least once.

Jack Are you happier now?

Victoria Much. Your insidious charm is working.

Jack kisses her hard on the mouth. Victoria strokes the back of his neck

Jack It's heaven. I'm sailing away.

Victoria (*feebly*) I don't think we should. Not so early in the morning.

Jack The morning's the best time. While you're full of energy.

Victoria It's not the bracelet. I really am very fond of you. (*She becomes very passionate*) It's so long since anyone made love to me.

Jack I understand.

They embrace again, Victoria the more vigorously of the two. Jack stands up and holds out his hand to her

Jack Let's go into your bedroom.

Victoria Oh, no. Philip wouldn't like it.

Jack He wouldn't know.

Victoria I'd feel terribly guilty. I wouldn't be comfortable.

Jack More comfortable than here. Making love on a sofa is such awful acrobatics.

Victoria stands up and draws Jack to her and on to the rug and they ease down to it

The Lights fade to Black-out

SCENE 5

A spotlight on Philip

Philip (*carrying his dispatch box*) A useful morning over. But I had a bit of a struggle with Sir Martin. There was the usual case of some potentate from the Middle East arrested for shop lifting. Sir Martin was all for letting British justice take its course. He hoped the fellow would be sent to jail as an example to the new breed of Barbary pirates looting Marks and Sparks. Sir Martin said, "We should never tamper with the law for political ends". I told him not to be so priggish. We've got a four hundred million pounds aircraft contract on the verge of being signed in the jolly shoplifter's country. "You're not going to make me responsible for losing all those jobs and to hell with British justice". I made him promise to arrange with the Home Office to have the man quietly deported. He didn't like it but he'll do it. It's fun being a minister. It must be still more so when you're in the Cabinet, though I'd rather be going round my farm at Lower Slaughter tonight than be at the Soviet Embassy. But you can't have the sweets of office without the penalties. My sandwich lunch (*He pats his dispatch box*) is bound to be an improvement on my fraught breakfast. I've always had a weakness for sandwiches. They've seen some exciting moments since that dissolute gambler and libertine the Earl of Sandwich invented them in the eighteenth century. He thought time eating meals away from the gaming tables was time wasted. He showed club servants how to put a slice of meat between two slices of bread and bring it on a plate so he wouldn't be interrupted at losing his fortune. That was his contribution to history. Apart from being the most corrupt and incompetent First Lord the Admiralty has ever had. His example to me was his towering political ambition. He let nothing, not even gambling, stand in the way of getting the ministerial rank he wanted. He was always happy to trade away his convictions though I'd never go quite so far as that. Those were the days when the Lords were almost as important as the Commons. They could overturn Commons' decisions and weren't afraid to. That was before the Lords had become a mausoleum in which political ghosts try to relive their pasts. I'd hate to be buried in it. I hope Victoria has been finding her day amusing. That might take the heat off me.

The Lights cross-fade to the sitting-room

SCENE 6

It is Friday lunch time

The red roses are where Victoria left them. Philip enters with his dispatch box and looks around and down the passage. He goes to the front door and opens it and calls out

Philip Jane, Jane. All clear.

He brings in Jane Trafford, holding her hand. She is younger than Victoria, wears glasses and a light appealing summer dress. Her hair is pulled back by a comb and she wears the diamond bracelet Philip has given her

Jane It's been so long since I've seen you. (*She puts her arms round him momentarily*)

Philip All of three minutes.

Jane I've been longing to see this place. Now I can picture you in it when we're not together. Are you sure it's safe?

Philip Couldn't be safer. (*He looks at his watch*) It's only just gone one. Victoria can't be back before five unless there's a cloudburst. I told you Maud's out for the day. So are the children.

Jane We don't have to be at the Ministry of Transport meeting until three forty-five. It's practically round the corner.

Philip Everything's perfect. It's our time out of life.

Jane I was always afraid of my flatmate bursting in. I'm hungry, Doggy.

Philip It's all in here. (*He opens his dispatch box and pulls out a linen napkin rolled round three sandwiches*) These sandwiches are fit for a queen— which you are.

Jane You're my Prince Charming.

Philip This one is caviar.

Jane Caviar's my favourite.

Philip All in wholemeal bread spread with margarine high in polyunsaturates. It can only do you good. *Wilton*'s made them.

Jane You are a silly Doggy, Philip, but sweet. And I'm thirsty too.

Philip Always keep a few half-bottles of pink champagne in the fridge for emergencies. This is one. (*He goes to the fridge*) The empties can wait in Her Majesty's Dispatch Box for later disposal.

Jane I wonder what the Queen would say if she knew?

Philip Probably laugh. The boxes she wades through are stuffed with dismally boring papers. It would be a nice surprise to find a half-bottle of pink champagne in one of them—full of course.

Jane (*looking at a picture on the wall*) Is this your place at Lower Slaughter?

Philip (*opening the champagne*) Yes. Abbey House. John Piper did it.

Jane How marvellous to live there.

Philip Ye-es-er. (*He puts the cork in his pocket and comes back with the bottle, carrying two glasses*) Let's have our picnic over here. (*He pours out the champagne and puts out the sandwiches*)

Jane What lovely red roses.

They start eating

Philip Good lord. They weren't here when I left this morning. Most unusual. Victoria prefers big, bosomy flowers.

Jane Your wife must have an admirer. Very keen judging from all those. Red roses are lovers' roses.

Philip Nonsense. (*Firmly*) She'd squash anything like that immediately. She's never looked at a man since we were married.

Jane Every woman at least looks at another man.

Philip Victoria wouldn't. Believes in the sanctity of the family. Sometimes I wish she didn't. It makes me feel a heel.

Jane I'm not the first? (*She pouts*)

Philip The passionate sex in my marriage wore out ages ago. A man must do something.

Jane Must he?

Philip Nature drives man to act as the prime mover in perpetuating the human race.

Jane Don't be so pompous. What a chauvinist you are.

Philip Nature's more concerned with efficiency on the production line than equality of the sexes.

Jane Speed, not romance.

Philip It takes a man thirty seconds to start a baby.

Jane I prefer a little longer.

Philip It's more serious for a woman to be promiscuous than a man. Men can and do flit from flower to flower.

Jane How pleasant for men. If you're right they have all the advantages.

Philip Not quite. Women are the bastion of the family. Their love is deeper and stronger. It lasts longer and is more satisfying.

Jane Your grand theory has been dented by the Pill, Doggy. Women are as free as men now.

Philip I'm sure Victoria doesn't think so. Not every woman is suddenly freed of thousands of years of psychological conditioning by easy contraception.

Jane Am I the proverbial bit on the side?

Philip I love you more in every way than I've ever loved anyone. I adore your understanding that my ambitions are not all selfish.

Jane It's more than sex?

Philip You conquered me with that clear way you wrote up the minutes. I can understand the meetings I've chaired.

Jane You always did.

Philip Not so well as I do now.

Jane It's a matter of confidence.

Philip You gave me much more. Brilliantly analysing those complicated reports civil servants deliberately try to confuse ministers with.

Jane I'm a civil servant.

Philip Yes. But the other civil servants hoped to blind me with befuddling expertise. You've made me twice their master.

Jane (*pleased*) It's because I love you, Doggy. It's the way your hair curls behind your ears. I know you'll be Prime Minister.

Philip Without you I don't think I'd even be in line for the Cabinet. I owe a lot to your brains and support.

Jane But I'm not bad looking, am I? Even though I got a first at Oxford.

Philip You're the world's most beautiful blue stocking.

Jane And I am a bit feminine? I love pretty jewellery.

Philip I love it on you.

Jane fingers the diamond bracelet appreciatively as it dangles on her wrist, and moves over to the sofa, carrying her glass. It is her second drink

Jane This pink champagne is perfection. And romantic.

Philip So are you. You've become my main reason for wanting to be alive. If you were gone I'd be finished.

Jane is sitting on the arm of the sofa. She unpins her hair and shakes it out. She takes off her glasses. Philip goes to stand beside the sofa, carrying his glass

Philip What an enchanting puppy you look.

Jane And you're a scrumptious doggy. Would you leave your wife for me?

Philip (*gulping*) If that were the only solution.

Jane It's the solution I want. I'm not going to let you go.

Philip I want to take you to the stars with me.

Jane (*laughing*) I think you're floating there on the champagne bubbles.

Philip I'm serious.

Jane So am I. Married men will say anything to get their way.

Philip I'm not like all the others.

Jane You're the first one I've felt was truly sincere. It's your character.

Philip I'll never let you down. It's for ever and for always.

Jane How do you know the sex would last if we were married? It didn't with your wife.

Philip It could never wear out with you. (*Reflectively*) But I'm bound to say it usually lasts longer with a mistress.

Jane Why?

Philip Unless you can live openly with her, the times you can see her are limited.

Jane So that keeps it fresh.

Philip What you have without effort palls fairly soon. And the risk of being found out heightens the excitement.

Jane Why didn't you take me to a hotel then?

Philip That would be elevating risk to folly. Someone might recognize me.

Jane You're not all that well known.

Philip (*miffed*) Don't be unkind. I've a high profile for the press.

The sun begins to fade as it clouds over

Jane It was unkind of you to say you'd rather have me as a mistress than as a wife.

Philip I didn't say that.

Jane It was the clear implication.

Philip Don't let's quarrel during our precious two hours.

Jane Not if you promise you'll share everything. If you get to be Prime Minister I want to still be at your side. It would be compensation for the sex running out.

Philip I promise. (*He kisses her passionately*) But give me time.

Jane A good, old fashioned scandal might dynamite you into my arms.

Philip It would dynamite my career if it came now during the Cabinet reshuffle.

Jane I was wishing it could happen when I was dreaming about us on my Easter holiday.

Philip I was dreaming about how marvellous an Easter holiday together would have been. Wondering what you were doing.

Jane The Prime Minister would never have sacked you then.

Philip She's very broad minded about that sort of thing. It's one of her best qualities. She even takes back renowned adulterers with illegitimate children.

Jane A philanderer's charter.

Philip Not at all. They're loyal and first class ministers. But her patience must be stretched to snapping point when the spotlight's on the people she gives new jobs to.

Jane Yes, we must be careful. It's our career now.

Philip Let's drink to that and to us.

They do so

Forever and for always.

Jane This champagne is making me deliciously woozy. I bet you give it to all the girls.

Philip (*drinking*) What else? (*He laughs*) It softens them up without their realizing.

They embrace thoroughly, Philip pushing her onto her back

Jane (*jumping up and holding out her hands*) I'm completely softened up. How wonderful we can make careless love at last without holding back from fear of interruption.

Philip I've been thinking of nothing else.

Jane Let's go into your bedroom.

Philip Oh, no. Victoria wouldn't like it.

Jane She wouldn't know.

Philip I'd feel terribly guilty. I wouldn't be comfortable.

Jane More comfortable than here. Making love on a sofa is such awful acrobatics.

Philip stands up and draws her to him and eases down to the rug to the accompaniment of lightning and thunder. Black-out

Scene 7

It is about six-thirty the same evening. A cloudy dusk

Victoria enters. She has changed into a cocktail dress suitable for an Embassy reception. She is elated and looks fondly at the roses, then sees the rumpled rug in front of the sofa and hurries to straighten it. The telephone rings. Victoria answers it

Victoria (*on the phone*) Treble two-six-two-nine-seven.... Yes, it's me speaking Mrs Brook-Green. Hyacinth's been cocaine sniffing ... Not just smoking pot ... Oh, how dreadful. ... No, I think that suspension to the end of term is quite lenient ... Thank you for not expelling her ... Yes, I know it's bad. I've tried to stop her being silly ... No, I don't think it's all the parents' fault.

Philip appears at the doorway carrying his dispatch box. He stops to listen

Schools have some duty to explain the dangers of drugs. This won't get into the newspapers, will it? It would be very bad publicity for my husband. ... One of the girls' father works for a tabloid. ... I didn't know you had parents like that ... I would never have guessed from all the name dropping at your school that you thought the children more important than the parents ... We're both being rude. The difference is I'm better at it. ... Goodbye, Mrs Brook-Green.

Philip enters

Philip I got the drift of that. Hyacinth's been caught smoking pot.
Victoria Cocaine. Mrs Brook-Green thinks it's largely your fault.
Philip My fault?
Victoria It's the parents' responsibility (*maliciously*)—particularly the fathers'—to impress on their children that playing around with drugs wrecks their lives.
Philip How could I know Hyacinth'd be such an idiot?
Victoria She says children wouldn't behave like that if parents set the right standards in the home.
Philip She would say that.
Victoria (*sweetly*) But your Minister of Education keeps saying the same.
Philip (*impatiently*) It's his stock in trade. No one takes any notice.
Victoria Don't tell the PM that.

Hyacinth comes in from the front door carrying a bag of books

Philip You bloody little fool. You promised this morning you wouldn't smoke pot. Now you're sniffing cocaine.
Victoria I think snorting is the technical term.
Hyacinth It was a scientific experiment.
Philip It was depraved debauchery.
Hyacinth Someone gave me a tiny packet of coke at a party.
Philip You're insane. Next stop addiction. You know where that ends.
Hyacinth But we didn't feel anything. It was a nothing.
Victoria It's not a nothing now. It's a disaster for you and it could be one for your father.
Hyacinth (*miserably*) I'm sorry, Mummy. And Daddy.
Victoria Mrs Brook-Green must be very experienced to know what you were doing.
Hyacinth She's caught other girls at it.
Philip St Marks must be one big Acid House party. What did she say?
Hyacinth That it was a disgrace for senior Markinas to behave like that. Especially if their fathers were ministers. (*She runs crying to her mother*)

Victoria I always thought Markinas was a silly name for girls at St Marks. Even Marxists would be better—and some of them are. Don't cry so.

Hyacinth (*through her sobs*) I'm so unhappy.

Philip I should damn well hope so. You're not crying from remorse. You're sorry for yourself because you've been caught. I'll speak to Mrs Brook-Green myself. (*He goes to the telephone*)

Victoria Her private number's on the pad.

Philip looks it up and dials

Don't be too hard on Hyacinth. She's had a going over from Mrs Brook-Green.

Philip (*on the phone*) Oh Mrs Brook-Green. It's Philip Grantly . . . I'm sorry my wife sounded cross. She was very upset . . . How nice of you . . . But please don't suspend Hyacinth. If it gets out it may damage the government . . . But it is something to do with you. It's not in the national interest . . . You can't possibly believe what you think are St Marks' interests are more important . . . In that case I shall certainly not be subscribing to the Appeal Fund for the new science building . . . Goodbye, Mrs Brook-Green. (*He puts down the telephone*) Hyacinth, have you got some work during your enforced absence?

Hyacinth (*picking up the bag of books she brought in*) Lots. In here.

Philip I hope it includes *King Lear* and what his daughters did to him.

Victoria Go to your room and start now. And get it into your head the harm you've done.

Hyacinth exits

Victoria Mrs Brook-Green's not a woman to be bullied.

Philip Blast her.

Victoria I'm amazed she's being so lenient.

Philip I feel like a drink. (*He pours himself a whisky*) How was Wimbledon?

Victoria Fine till the thunder and lightning, though that was exciting. How was your day?

Philip I found the thunder an exhilarating background too.

Victoria Where were you?

Philip At a boring meeting at the Ministry of Transport. But it wasn't a bad day on the whole. (*Smiling at his thoughts he sits down, pleased with himself*)

Victoria I'd like a drink too, darling. Is there any pink champagne?

Philip (*getting up and going to the fridge*) Yes. There's one half-bottle here.

Victoria How odd. I'm sure there were three last night. Where could the others have gone?

Philip I can't think. Perhaps Maud took them to her mother.

Victoria Ridiculous. Anyway pretend I'm your girl friend.

Philip You're my eternal girl friend. (*He brings the champagne and one glass and opens the bottle. Then he sits on the sofa*)

Victoria That's nice.

Philip What a moment for Hyacinth to be an idiot. The PM has warned everyone the government can't take any more scandals. Ministers' private lives must be impeccable for the time being.

Victoria They can play around later. When the public have got over the last scandal.

Philip The timing would be better. There's also a suggestion you've got the hang of: if ministers get into scrapes, it will undermine the new campaign the Government is launching.

Victoria What's that?

Philip That behaviour in the nation is determined by behaviour in the family.

Victoria So I was right. It's the Minister of Education's bizarre new policy. The sins of the children will be visited on the parents. Mrs Brook-Green will like that.

Philip I'm damned if I'd like it. I haven't slaved away for years to have my political career destroyed by my selfish children playing the fool.

Victoria sits on the arm of the sofa and kisses him. She touches the back of his neck

Victoria I never noticed before how attractively your hair curls behind your ears.

Philip (*startled*) Er, what? What a peculiar thing to say.

Victoria I'm sure other women have said it.

Philip Not that I know of. (*He changes the subject*) Where did those roses come from?

Victoria A present from you. You owe me seventy pounds. But I won't ask for it now. I got them on the way back from Wimbledon.

Philip On the way back from Wimbledon! That's rum. But I . . .

Victoria I had a sudden impulse to imagine you were romantic as you used to be. I'm sorry if that upsets you.

Philip No, no. Not at all.

Victoria While I was in Bond Street this morning I saw a divine looking diamond bracelet at *Cartier*.

Philip What about it?

Victoria It made me feel I could be exotic again.

Philip Like those impulsive roses perhaps.

Hyacinth returns. She has been crying. She runs to Philip

Hyacinth Daddy, I'm so sorry.

Philip puts his arm around her

I know I was wrong. I'll never do it again. This time I really promise.

Philip It was damned inconsiderate. It could wreck my promotion prospects. But I suppose we all do silly things at times.

Victoria (*with a trace of amusement*) Yes, we do. And at any age.

Hyacinth I don't see what it's got to do with politics, Daddy.

Victoria Your father's scared stiff of anything which could remotely stop him being in the Cabinet. He's worked so hard for it.

Philip It may seem absurd but that's the danger of it getting into the papers.

Hyacinth You could ask them not to put it in.

Victoria We know some newspaper proprietors quite well.

Philip Most modern proprietors are terrified of being accused of censorship if they suppress stories about their friends. All their employees leak to *Private Eye*.

Hyacinth I can't think why newspapers should print nasty things about me. No one's heard of me.

Philip You're my daughter. Journalists claim the right to publish any item they can dig up to discredit me or my family. It's known as the public interest.

Victoria I can see why the public are interested. I adore Nigel Dempster's tittle-tattle. Particularly if it's about my friends.

Hyacinth (*upset*) But, Daddy, writing about my being suspended from St Marks might be funny. It can't be in the public interest.

Philip It is for our slimy self-righteous press. The innuendo is that I haven't brought my family up properly. So I'm unfit to be a Minister.

Hyacinth How thrilling to be an innocent victim of parental neglect.

Victoria It's not funny, Hyacinth. Drug taking is deadly serious. It worries the Prime Minister almost more than anything else.

Philip It could influence her thinking on the re-shuffle.

Victoria I can believe that.

Philip Smears against ministers are like points for road offences.

Victoria One too many and you lose your licence to govern.

Philip It wasn't always so. Lloyd George was notorious for groping every passable woman under forty.

Hyacinth Lloyd George was the Prime Minister who married his secretary.

Philip Ye-es. After his wife was dead.

Victoria How did he get away with behaving like a goat?

Philip In Lloyd George's day the press didn't treat the private lives of politicians as soft porn.

Hyacinth Is there no way of getting the press to leave a politician alone now?

Philip The threat of a libel action can stop them.

Victoria Does that work if what they've printed is true?

Philip If they can't prove it. And the victim brazens it out. It requires nerve but it can be worth the risk. The greater the truth the greater the libel damages.

Victoria (*slowly*) I see.

Philip But it obviously wouldn't work in Hyacinth's case. They'd subpoena Mrs Brook-Green to give evidence.

Hyacinth (*contemptuously*) She'd never tell a lie. I'm going to get something to eat before Julian comes back and hogs it all.

Hyacinth goes down the hall

Philip The cocaine business is pretty serious. Not only for me blast it. But for her.

Victoria She's had the fright of her life.

Philip You're not afraid of any lasting harm?

Victoria Not if we support her and think more of her concerns than our own.

Philip (*looking at his watch*) Good. That's the loving mother's department. Do you think I need to shave?

Victoria Come closer. (*She feels his cheek*) Where are we having dinner?

Philip I've booked a table at the *Garrick*.

Victoria Why not *Wilton's*?

Philip (*blanching*) I had a quick lunch off their sandwiches today. I feel like sitting among those wonderful Zoffanys in the coffee room. I imagine myself back in the civilized eighteenth century.

Victoria Inhaling the stench of the smelly open drains.

Philip There's nothing wrong with the plumbing at the *Garrick* now. I prefer it to *Whites*. They all think they're so socially superior there.

Victoria All right. The *Garrick*. Then you've no need to shave.

Philip Sure?

Victoria The Russians won't notice. Nor will the intellectually superior members at the *Garrick*. The time's long gone when you shaved for me.

Philip Oh dear, the needle's back in your voice. It was there this morning too.

Victoria Sorry. But you might change your suit. It looks as though you've been rolling in the hay.

Philip (*looking guiltily at his suit with which there is nothing wrong*) Hay? Just needs pressing. (*He starts to smooth his coat*) I'll be right back.

Hyacinth, chicken leg in hand, appears as Philip exits

Hyacinth Is it OK with Daddy?

Victoria He's dreadfully worried about the newspapers. That's natural.

Hyacinth Funny. One never thinks about one's parents being worried. They seem so secure.

Victoria Hardly anyone really feels secure.

Hyacinth Having a lot of money must help.

Victoria If you're unhappy it's marginally nicer to drink champagne in a comfortable house than half a pint of bitter in a back street pub.

Hyacinth What a gloomy thought.

Victoria No, realistic as Julian would say. The fates are lurking around for all of us. They make no distinction between rich and poor.

Hyacinth (*noticing*) What lovely flowers, Mummy.

Victoria Yes. Daddy gave them me.

Hyacinth Good Lord! It's not like him.

Victoria He must have been feeling romantic.

Hyacinth Was it a surprise?

Victoria Quite surprising for both of us.

Hyacinth Have you got something to celebrate?

Victoria If those fates are in a good mood.

Hyacinth By the way you never told me what your day was like, Mummy. My awful day blotted the thought of everyone else's out.

Victoria Lovely, really lovely. One of the nicest days of my life. Not even the storm at Wimbledon spoiled it.

Hyacinth (*glumly*) Who's in the Men's Finals?

Victoria No one knows yet. They stopped altogether for rain somewhere in the third set. I can't remember where they'd got to. (*Happily*) I was thinking of other things.

Hyacinth You are awful, Mummy. Fancy not knowing the score.

The telephone rings

Victoria I'll answer it. (*She picks up the telephone and listens*) Hallo, hallo. . . . Oh, it's someone in a coinbox. It's gone off.

Hyacinth That's always happening.

Victoria Especially since British Telecom was privatised.

The telephone rings

Victoria Drat it. (*She answers it*) Who is that? Can't hear anything . . . Now it's gone dead again. The miracles of modern communications will never cease.

Philip enters wearing a different suit

You've been quick.

Philip We'd better go. Or the Labour MPs will have scoffed all the caviar.

Victoria Goodbye, Hyacinth. (*She picks up her coat and kisses Hyacinth*)

Philip (*to Hyacinth*) Good night, Hyacinth. (*He kisses her*) You're still my favourite daughter.

Hyacinth You've only got one, Daddy.

Philip Exactly. (*He laughs*)

Hyacinth I'm truly sorry, Daddy.

Philip (*going out with Victoria*) We won't be very late.

The telephone rings. Hyacinth goes to answer but Philip rushes back. Victoria returns

Philip Give it to me. It may be Number Ten. (*He picks up the phone*) Hallo, hallo. It's gone dead. Must be someone in a coin box. They don't have them at Number Ten. Expect it's safe to go out.

Philip and Victoria go out of the front door

Hyacinth lingers for a moment, reflectively, then goes out. She's just gone when the telephone rings. She returns and picks it up

Hyacinth (*on the phone*) Six-two-nine-seven . . . Oh, Julian. They've just gone. Was it you trying to get through just now? . . . Where are you? . . . What on earth are you doing at Bow Street police station? . . . Did you hit the policeman? . . . That's your story . . . Why won't they say when they'll let you out? . . . Were there any reporters there? . . . And photographers! . . . You're a bloody exhibitionist . . . Yes, you are, Julian. . . . Goodbye.

(*She puts the telephone down. It rings again. She picks it up*) Six-two-nine-seven. . . . My father's not here. . . . Did you say the *News of the World*? . . . You could try again later. (*She puts the telephone down and faces the audience*) Poor Daddy—What a fucking mess.

CURTAIN

ACT II

SCENE 1

The Garrick Club. Evening

Philip is sitting in one of two chairs under the main staircase. He has a balloon glass of brandy in his hand

Philip The Russians have the best caviar in the world and the worst champagne. Still the vodka's genuine. It put our hosts in a merry mood. Their new Foreign Minister was very keen to please. Compared inspectors verifying nuclear arms reductions to cricket umpires. He overdid it by boning up on the latest score in the Test. Tactless with England making the usual hash of it. But full marks for trying. Must be part of the *glasnost* show. It was a nice surprise meeting up with Jack and Mary here at the *Garrick Club*. Though Victoria was noticeably more pleased to see Mary than to see Jack. I wonder if he's done something to upset her. Victoria's been in an odd mood since breakfast. She couldn't have known about Jane and me at the flat. That happened afterwards. She'd blow her top if she knew about Jane's diamond bracelet. I wonder what the PM is planning. If I get in the Cabinet I could be in the running for PM myself. Whatever job I had I'd make enough splash to keep in the public eye. Not like that anonymous fellow, John Major. He'll never make the top. Why ever does it take Victoria so long to get ready? Jack drove Mary home ten minutes ago. He's coming back later to talk to someone from Newmarket about a horse. I might ask him if he'd let me have a dabble in it too. I'd trust Jack's judgement on horses more than on the women he larks about with.

Victoria appears with her evening coat on

Oh, there you are darling.
Victoria I couldn't bear to leave the Ladies. It's like an eighteenth-century boudoir.
Philip I thought you were a bit off-hand with Jack tonight. I hope he didn't notice.
Victoria I shouldn't think so. He's too captivated by his own charm to grasp it might not be captivating everyone else.
Philip I thought you liked him.
Victoria I'm very fond of him.
Philip With reservations?
Victoria Not serious ones. I just wonder whether he cares deeply about anyone or anything.
Philip It's true he's cynical about politics.

Victoria And everything else.

Philip That's the difference between him and me. I'm one hundred per cent ambitious but I also mind like mad what happens to the country.

Victoria I couldn't have lived with you all this time and not discovered that.

Philip What a marvellous thing to say.

Victoria I don't always agree with your heroine and politics is not my favourite world.

Philip I'm sorry. But I mean every word about Britain rising from the ashes now that people aren't frightened of the trade unions any more. They may not like her but the Prime Minister's done one hell of a good job. She got Britain punching twice her weight with the US President, the German Chancellor and the rest of them. She's restored our pride. She's tamed the unions. She's let private enterprise free to create the highest standard of living we've ever had. Most of the men in the Cabinet hate her and want her out. But she's our Joan of Arc. If they burned her they'd soon wish they hadn't.

Victoria Yes, yes. Don't go on so. I know you want to be in the Cabinet for what you think you can do there. It isn't only because it would make you grander.

Philip Thanks.

Victoria It's because you're a believer that I love you—unless you hurt me too much.

Philip You're too sensible to be easily hurt.

Victoria I'm a woman.

Philip Unfortunately, I'm a man.

Philip and Victoria exit as the Lights fade

SCENE 2

The sitting-room. It is night

Julian enters followed by Maud, carrying a cup of coffee. He turns on the lights. Maud gives him the coffee and then draws the curtains

Julian Thanks, Maud. It was really good of you to cook me the bacon and eggs.

Maud I was lucky to get here in time to take the pan out of your hand.

Julian I was lucky the police let me go at nine thirty. Sometimes they hold them until after the last buses and tubes have gone.

Maud You got melted butter all over my kitchen floor.

Julian (*holding up his finger to his mouth*) Shhh. No butter for cooking in this house, Maud.

Maud My family have always been healthy eating things Mr Grantly says we shouldn't.

Julian That's before there were statistics to prove you couldn't possibly have been. Capitalist statistics are lies to keep the working classes quiet.

Maud I'm not working class. My father was a death knocker.

Julian What's that?

Maud A life insurance collector. Collecting from the working classes . . .

Julian The working class are the salt of the earth.

Maud (*sniffing*) They cheer when someone wins the football pools. But they're full of envy if he makes money by hard work. Working class, my eye.

Julian You can't be against the working class, Maud.

Maud You don't want to worship them as plaster saints, mi duck. Like politicians, there's good and there's bad.

Julian (*despairingly*) I was helping the working class to overthrow capitalist society—so everyone can be free.

Maud You've been reading too many books by professors. Like that Karl Marx I saw on the telly smoking cigars.

Julian Marx is dead.

Maud He wasn't the other night.

Julian It wasn't fact, it was fiction.

Maud Fiction's what it is. Those professors persuade fools to make a dream world. Then any complaints and the police march you off.

Julian We live in a police state, Maud. Two policemen grabbed me, then one of them hit me with his truncheon.

Maud You're looking quite well on it. I can't listen to any more of your nonsense.

Maud exits with the coffee cup

Hyacinth enters in her dressing gown

Hyacinth They'll be back soon.

Julian (*jumping up and shadow boxing*) Seconds out of the ring. Another round of rows coming up.

Hyacinth You're an ape. You want to get yourself all over the newspapers and muck up Daddy's chances.

Julian It wasn't my fault. It was the police's.

Hyacinth It was your fault for being there. The *News of the World* rang up after I'd spoken to you.

Julian They're quick off the mark. And they don't come out till Sunday.

Hyacinth It might just have been about me but I don't think so.

Julian You!

Hyacinth Mrs Brook-Green caught some of us snorting cocaine. I've been suspended from school.

Julian Shit. That's great from Miss Goody Two Shoes.

Hyacinth I'm sure she won't tell the press.

Julian You bet some slimy sneak from your po-faced school will. They could get fifty quid from Nigel Dempster.

Hyacinth They're not as despicable as that.

Julian I might blow it myself. That'd really put the boot in for Dad.

Hyacinth You couldn't be such a bastard.

Julian Why not? He said he'd cut off my allowance if I went on the protest march.

Hyacinth Don't you like Mummy and Daddy?
Julian Mummy's fine, though she's practically brainless.
Hyacinth I love and admire them both. I'm frightfully ashamed of letting them down.
Julian You can't admire Dad. He's a low level politician on the make.
Hyacinth He's not. He's been jolly decent to you.
Julian I suppose apart from politics he's got some good points. I'm fond of the old fraud in a way.

Victoria and Philip come through the front door

Hyacinth Daddy will be jolly pleased to hear ...
Philip What will I be pleased to hear?
Julian (*nervously*) Oh, hallo, Dad. Hallo, Ma.
Hyacinth Did you have a good time at the *Garrick*?
Victoria Lovely.

The telephone rings. Julian goes to it. Philip gets between Julian and the telephone

Philip Keep away from the telephone. It might be Number Ten. (*He picks up the telephone*) Hallo ... why shouldn't he have got home all right? ... No you can't speak to him now. Try tomorrow. (*He hangs up the telephone*) That man had a voice like a sinister conspirator. (*He turns to Julian*) What the hell have you been up to?
Julian It was the demo I told you about. The police made an unprovoked attack. I was pushed from behind on to them.
Victoria (*concerned*) Did they hurt you?
Philip I hope so. I'd like to kick him all the way to his bloody Poly.
Julian Thanks, Dad. I wasn't hurt, Ma. A bit of a bruise here and there. And roughing up from two Fascist police pigs Dad would approve of.
Victoria (*going towards Julian*) My poor darling. What brutes. They ought to be prosecuted.
Philip The question is will the little swine be prosecuted?
Julian I've got to go to Bow Street Magistrates' Court when it opens tomorrow morning.
Philip Oh God. I begged you not to put that silly demo above my career. You're too conceited to think of anyone but yourself.
Hyacinth That's true.
Julian Shut up, Hyacinth. You're no bloody saint.
Philip At least she cares about me.
Julian (*sneering*) You're afraid of not being promoted. What does it matter? There's no difference between any of you bourgeois mediocrities.
Victoria (*going to sit down*) Oh, Julian, don't be so nasty to your father.
Julian (*walking up and down; haranguing*) He asked for it. The publicity will draw attention to our cause. There were lots of television cameras. Dad doesn't matter historically this much. (*He snaps his fingers*)
Philip You little bastard. You don't care a damn about letting me down.
Julian The police were waiting for us. Did you tip them off?

Philip I warned the Home Secretary. One of your friends probably tipped off the police as well.

Julian They wouldn't do that.

Philip You have the publicity value of being my son. Otherwise they must despise you as a shallow young twerp with too much money. It won't be a problem for you after I've cut your allowance.

Julian Not true. They admire my grasp of revolutionary theory and why defending anti-poll tax marchers is a part of it.

Philip That wouldn't stop one of them pushing you on to a policeman. The story's more newsworthy if you're arrested.

Julian They'd never be so dishonourable.

Victoria I'm sure they're all nice young people like Julian.

Philip (*with his voice raised*) Julian isn't nice. He's vicious and disloyal.

Julian (*shouting*) Who wouldn't be with a father like you?

Hyacinth All that shouting nearly made me forget. The *News of the World* rang just after you went.

Philip What the hell do they want?

Hyacinth I don't know. I told them to try again later.

Philip It's either Julian who's been arrested for attacking the police. Or you for being suspended for snorting cocaine.

Julian Hyacinth is typical of the collapse of capitalist society.

Hyacinth Russian soldiers taken prisoner in Afghanistan were on heroin. Russia's got a huge drug problem.

Julian Probably because they're diluting Communism to suck up to the West.

Victoria A truce. A truce. Leave it alone, and go to bed children. I want to talk to your father about something privately.

Julian Goodnight.

Hyacinth Goodnight.

Julian and Hyacinth start down the hall

Victoria Goodnight, you monsters.

Philip Goodnight Hyacinth. Goodnight, Trotsky.

Julian Goodnight, Oswald Mosley.

Julian gives a fascist salute as they exit

The telephone rings. Victoria answers it

Victoria (*on the phone*) Treble two-six-two-nine-seven ... Yes this is Mrs Grantly speaking ... Hold on a moment, I'll see if he's back ... I know nothing about it, and I don't believe it. (*She puts her hand over the receiver*) It's the *News of the World*.

Philip What are they on about? Hyacinth, or Julian, or both?

Victoria Neither. They say they've got a story, a very solid one, about you and Miss Trafford.

Philip (*furiously*) Give me that telephone. I'll deal with them.

Victoria (*taking her hand off the receiver*) My husband's just coming.

Philip grabs the telephone. Victoria goes back to the sofa

Philip (*on the phone*) Hallo ... Nothing improper at all. How dare you
suggest it? ... We may have been in a restaurant ... That would be after
working late. Nothing extraordinary about that ... Not every couple in a
restaurant is having an affair ... Holding hands? You've got a filthy mind
... Not just holding hands? I warn you, if you print anything remotely
suggesting something improper between Miss Trafford and myself, you'll
have to pay so much in libel damages it'll sink your gutter newspaper
below the sea ... Why didn't you check with me first? ... Oh, that's what
you are doing. OK ... So you won't decide to print anything yet if I speak
to your editor before twelve o'clock in the morning? ... (*Vehemently*)
Goodnight. (*He puts down the telephone*) That was a near run thing. They
were planning to print malicious lies about Miss Trafford and me. I can
straighten out the *News of the World* in the morning. The Editor's a friend
of mine.

Victoria But it's true, isn't it?

Philip Ridiculous! Miss Trafford's a very respectable girl and a good
Private Secretary. Nothing more.

Victoria So you say. (*She opens her handbag and takes out the memo. She
reads*) "Important memo! I love the way your hair curls behind your ears,
doggy ..."

Philip squirms

This bit I found truly fascinating, "We must get our evening drink
together so I can show off our diamond bracelet."

Philip Where did you find that?

Victoria In one of your pockets.

Philip You're as bad as I am.

Victoria But you're more vulnerable. How could you lie to that poor
newspaper man?

Philip I had to.

Victoria You should have said, "I love Miss Trafford. I have given her a
diamond bracelet. She calls me doggy and I'm going to take her to the
stars with me".

Philip (*embarrassed*) I've never said anything about taking her to the stars.
That isn't in the memo is it?

Victoria It's what you used to say to me. I assume you've used the same
material with her. You told me Churchill said "If you've got a good
speech, stick to it".

Philip That's politics. Not real life.

Victoria What do you propose I should do while you are on the way to the
stars with Miss Trafford wearing her expensive diamond bracelet?

Philip It wasn't expensive.

Victoria How much did it cost?

Philip Not a lot. About three thousand pounds. Why do you want to know?

Victoria I just wanted a benchmark. Three thousand pounds means you're
getting in deep.

Philip This is all jumping the gun. We haven't even——

Victoria (*interrupting*) Found out if you've been promoted? You won't be if this gets out while the re-shuffles are swirling in the PM's head. How far has this gone?

Philip It's difficult to explain.

Victoria Not if you tell the truth.

Philip I don't know what the truth is.

Victoria That's normal for a politician.

Philip At the *Garrick* you said how sincere I was.

Victoria I also said I'd always love you unless you hurt me too much. I'm badly hurt now. Have you promised to marry her, for instance?

Philip Not exactly.

Victoria You've promised her with enough qualification to leave you a get out?

Philip We agreed not to do anything precipitate. She doesn't want to damage my career. She's very caring.

Victoria She cares all right. If you get into the Cabinet, she'll take you. If you don't you're finished and I can keep you.

Philip You're trying to make it sordid. She loves me for myself.

Victoria Piffle. I know that kind of woman. She's glamour struck for power; and preening herself as she goes to Buckingham Palace. If she thinks that's off the menu, you'll be off it too—however prettily your hair curls.

Philip (*humbly*) I'm sorry, Victoria.

Victoria You're not sorry at all. Like Hyacinth you're just sorry you've been found out. Don't think I haven't known about some of the others.

Philip Just innocent flirtations.

Victoria Like that nauseating little actress who used to look at you with goo-goo eyes and say, "Oh, Mr Grantly, you're so witty. You'd make a wonderful playwright. I'd love to be in a play by you".

Philip (*cringing*) Lay off.

Victoria And there was the merry young widow you advised on her investments. You gave her enough advice at all hours of the day and night to send her bankrupt several times over.

Philip She did very well out of it.

Victoria So did you.

Philip But you never said anything.

Victoria You were like an adolescent prey to his sex drive. Sex was easier for you to get then. You weren't so desperate about it.

Philip My minor excursions never threatened our marriage.

Victoria But now you're in the Last Chance saloon. Your current infatuation is the most dangerous yet.

Philip I don't see why.

Victoria You're convincing yourself it's the great love of your life; that you're on the verge of a magic new beginning in the Cabinet; that a new and invincible Philip is going to astound the world, flashing a brand new sword.

Philip You haven't got it right at all.

Victoria I have, Philip. Your dream is the noble excuse you give yourself for your appalling treachery.

Philip That's a harsh description for a situation thousands get into.

Victoria It's still treachery. Almost as bad as those cowards in the cabinet with knives poised behind the PM's back. At least I know about it.

Philip I try to warn her but she says I'm just making mischief.

Victoria If they strike it'll be the most shattering bereavement of your life.

Philip Surely there must have been something for you in all our years together.

Victoria The constituency? Parading like an idiot in a beauty contest in front of those beastly selection conferences your dreary party holds.

Philip That was to judge whether you would make a good MP's wife.

Victoria It was so that the women could make catty remarks and the men could leer.

Philip You used to say how amusing it was.

Victoria That was because I loved you, you fool. I loathed it.

Philip tries to speak

Stop. I've been bottling this up for years. And when you got adopted after ten tries, unending deserts of boredom opened up. Eating disgusting dinners, sitting next to constituency committee members, their faces overblown by drink and self-importance.

Philip They weren't all boring.

Victoria You didn't have to listen to their ghastly golfing stories. And pretend not to notice when they demonstrated how their ball rolled up the fairway by stroking my thigh. (*She strokes her thigh*)

Philip But you seemed to enjoy the election meetings.

Victoria Listening to your speeches and laughing at your jokes as if I'd never heard them before.

Philip They're pretty good as election speeches go.

Victoria At the thirtieth repetition they're not. You can't explain anything complicated.

Philip Clarity is one of my greatest assets.

Victoria You counter your opponent's case with insults.

Philip They do the same.

Victoria I dare say, but I don't have to listen to them. Listening to you, I'm puzzled anyone ever votes Tory.

Philip The Prime Minister?

Victoria She's not a Tory. She's a radical revolutionary. That's why non-Tories vote for her. She terrifies the bumbling old Establishment Tories.

Philip It's certainly thanks to her we go on winning.

Victoria But not to the awful canvassing when we annoy people who just want to watch *EastEnders* undisturbed.

Philip (*abashed*) I didn't know you hated the constituency so much.

Victoria See how your wide eyed Miss Trafford likes it.

Philip Why bring her into it?

Victoria I thought that was what you planned to do. Tell Miss Trafford it doesn't finish with the Constituency. The House of Commons is far worse.

Philip It's the most entertaining part.

Victoria Parliament is hell for marriages. No quiet home life like ordinary couples. Being polite to revolting MPs!

Philip Is there no-one you like in Parliament?

Victoria A few. I have a soft spot for Jack.

Philip He thinks it's just a jolly joke putting MP after his name. He's only on the fringe of politics.

Victoria Perhaps he has more entertaining diversions. (*She smiles to herself*)

Philip The fast women and slow horses syndrome.

Victoria (*putting her hand on her hair and preening herself*) Actually, I quite like the Chief Whip. He fancies me in a gentlemanly sort of way.

Philip It could be useful.

Victoria I've been delicately playing on him to nudge the Prime Minister in your favour. He's going into the Cabinet himself.

Philip (*his political interest temporarily overcoming his worries*) What as?

Victoria I shouldn't have mentioned it. Keeping confidences is an invaluable weapon for women without careers.

Philip What's he say about me?

Victoria You're a borderline case. The PM wants another reasonably capable minister in the Cabinet who'll make no trouble.

Philip She's my heroine but I'm not a yes man.

Victoria You're not a boat rocker. The new man must have good judgment, a safe pair of hands and an impeccable home life. A bit dicey at the moment, I would think.

Philip (*miserably*) I've got to act fast.

Victoria You've got till tomorrow morning to decide. Or you'll be on your way to nowhere with Miss Trafford.

Philip Or we all lie our heads off and warn the *News of the World* we'll give them hell if they print anything.

Victoria That's the good old Philip fighting spirit.

Philip It still wouldn't get us off the hook over Julian and Hyacinth.

Victoria You might get away with them if your Miss Trafford weren't around.

Philip Yes, three out of three hitting the fan in one day would make me look more in need of advice than able to give it to the Cabinet.

Victoria It all depends on your floosie being prepared to deny everything.

Philip It would be an awful lot to ask.

Victoria You mean after all you've promised her.

Philip (*sheepishly*) You know how it is.

Victoria You're in the dilemma of all decent men with the same commitments to two women.

Philip Well ...

Victoria I suppose you could always hop off safely in six months after you'd got your Cabinet job. If you get it.

Philip That wouldn't be fair to you.

Victoria That's your problem.

Philip You don't deserve all this, Victoria. Christ, what a muddle I've made.

Victoria You'd better start thinking your way through the maze.

Philip I will. I need some second opinions.

Victoria It'll have to be fast with the *News of the World* waiting to pounce tomorrow morning.

Philip We need a lawyer—important enough to come the heavy with them.

Victoria Sir Edgar Wiseman.

Philip Brilliant. Would you get hold of him? He's always had a weakness for you.

Victoria OK. I'll ask him to come early in the morning.

Philip There's a risk in having a lawyer.

Victoria Why?

Philip You have to tell him the truth.

Victoria You said earlier you didn't know what the truth was.

Philip That was about what my real feelings were. I know the facts.

Victoria Wait till you see what Sir Edgar and I can do with the facts.

Philip I'm afraid Miss Trafford will have to be here too.

Victoria The Scarlet Secretary's your responsibility.

Philip And we need someone who knows how the world works.

Victoria Jack's our man. He can stand back from it all and give us disinterested advice.

Philip I'll pop back to the *Garrick*. I long to hear what Jack thinks. He's bound to be still talking about his horse.

Victoria Darling, good luck. (*She suddenly kisses him*)

Philip (*responding*) For ever and for always.

Victoria You can't be that for two at once.

Philip If you hadn't found that memo I'd have had a damn good try.

Philip goes through the front door

Victoria goes to the telephone as the Lights cross-fade to the "Garrick Club"

SCENE 3

The "Garrick Club". Later that night

Philip and Jack enter the alcove at the "Garrick" with a bottle of champagne and two silver mugs. They sit in armchairs

Jack We'll be fine here. There's no one about to disturb us.

Philip Good. (*He lifts his mug*) I can do with this.

Jack Champagne always tastes better in silver mugs.

Philip Agreed. I'm glad you were still in the Club. Victoria was very keen I should talk to you urgently.

Jack What's the matter?

Philip She thinks it's something you'll understand.

Jack Why?

Philip She's terribly upset.

Jack About me?

Philip Why on earth should she be upset about you?

Jack About Hyacinth?

Philip Not really. Not even about Julian.

Jack What's the Revolutionary done now?

Philip He's up before the Beak tomorrow morning for assaulting the police.

Jack Don't worry about minor things like that. They won't wreck the brilliant career you've made after overcoming the handicap of being a rich Etonian.

Philip She's upset about something which goes much deeper.

Jack She's not having an affair with someone?

Philip Don't be a chump. The *News of the World* just rang up. They're on to a story that I'm having an affair with my Private Secretary, Jane Trafford.

Jack That's a blockbuster.

Philip I've stalled them for the moment. But Victoria's creating hell.

Jack You couldn't have been silly enough to admit it.

Philip She found a note from Jane this morning. It was somewhat compromising.

Jack A high grade Civil Servant ought to know you should never write a love letter. Unless it's so ambiguous you wouldn't mind it being read out in Court.

Philip There was something in it about a diamond bracelet.

Jack (*nervously*) Diamond bracelet? Surely you never gave a diamond bracelet to Miss Trafford?

Philip Certainly I did.

Jack You might have been wiser to give one to Victoria as well.

Philip Why?

Jack No woman is pleased at being left out of the diamond bracelet awards.

Philip I wish your idiotic suggestion she was having an affair was right. She'd be more tolerant.

Jack She's not the type who'd ever do that.

Philip Much too strait-laced.

Jack Surely you can rely on her to do the decent thing.

Philip I don't know what the decent thing is. Jane thinks I'm going to marry her. She's mad keen for it.

Jack You'd be a bloody idiot to wreck your career over a bimbo.

Philip She's not a bimbo. She's full of brains. She makes me happier than anyone ever has.

Jack That kind of happiness dies as fast as it sprouts. Believe me.

Philip Despite your undoubted experience, I don't.

Jack You'll have to ditch her if you want Victoria's support to brazen it out with the *News of the World*.

Philip I don't know whether she's going for the kill or not. Just before I left she was hinting if we could silence the press—and I got in to the Cabinet—I could decide what to do in six months or so.

Jack Your lady friend might welcome that. She'd prefer the bird in hand to have some feathers on it.

Philip Jane loves me for myself. As I love her.

Jack Of course, of course. But it puts you in an appalling mess.

Philip What's your advice, Jack?

Jack Send for Sir Edgar Wiseman. Everyone does when they're in a jam.

Philip Victoria's trying to get him to the flat tomorrow morning. Victoria wants you, too. She relies on you for what she calls disinterested advice.

Jack She's quite right. I'm very fond of you both.

Philip You're the best friend I have, Jack, and the most loyal. And, Jack, you've got a nose for covering up awkward situations. Let's finish this champagne.

Jack No, no, I'm driving.

Philip (*pouring the remainder of the bottle into his mug*) By the way, how did you get on with that filly?

Jack I bought it. Would you like a share in it? You can have a leg.

Philip How much?

Jack Sixty-two thousand, five hundred guineas.

Philip I'll think about it. I'd rather share a horse with you than a woman.

Jack I'm off. See you in the morning.

Philip Yes. I'll ring you as soon as I know when Sir Edgar is coming.

Jack I hope he comes early. I've got a runner in the three o'clock at Lingfield.

Philip (*as Jack goes*) You always did put horses before women.

Jack exits

The Lights cross-fade to the sitting-room

SCENE 4

The sitting-room. It is Saturday morning

Used breakfast things are on the trolley. Maud is polishing the dining table

Victoria comes in wearing a dressing-gown. She puts a notepad on a table. The roses are nowhere to be seen

Victoria Oh, good morning, Maud. How's your mother?

Maud Much better than expected thank you Mrs Grantly. The flowers were lovely. She said to thank you both ever so much.

Victoria There'll be some people coming in. We'll need coffee for five. It's a crisis morning.

Maud I heard about it on the news.

Victoria (*alarmed*) We're done for already then.

Maud Why? It said an announcement was expected this weekend about government changes. Isn't that what Mr Grantly has been faffing about?

Victoria (*relieved*) Yes.

Maud He'll always be as right as a cart. He's got that lovely Abbey Farm at Lower Slaughter. He could go back to running the family bank.

Victoria Politicians think their life is over if they're no longer in the public eye. It makes Mr Grantly happy.

Maud My mam used to push Dad into the chequers tournaments at the local. Said a man must have a hobby. It must be the same for Mr Grantly.

Victoria You couldn't have put it better, Maud. Politics is a wonderful hobby for Mr Grantly, but unlike your father's chequers we all get dragged into it.

Hyacinth enters from the hall, carrying an empty book bag and wearing a hat

Hyacinth Oh Mummy, I'm just off.

Victoria Where are you going?

Hyacinth London Library. They've put some history books aside for me.

Victoria (*delighted*) I'm glad you're so keen. What are they about?

Hyacinth John Wilkes and the Medmenham (*pronounced mednam*) Monks and the Hellfire Club. Black magic and orgies. Bogus priests seducing bogus nuns on the altar. Leading politicians having fun with sex.

Victoria (*doubtfully*) Is that important?

Hyacinth It tells you how politics have changed.

Victoria (*slowly*) Does it really?

Hyacinth Hope Daddy gets good news from Number Ten.

Victoria So do I. We're about to have a meeting. The press may be difficult.

Hyacinth I'm awfully sorry. Julian and I are thoughtless pests.

Victoria You've got a glorious future, darling. Don't wreck it by being foolish.

Hyacinth I won't go down that primrose path again. I never realized before how much you loved me, Mummy.

Victoria I do, I do. (*She hugs Hyacinth*) You're much more valuable to me than your father's political career. But don't tell him.

Hyacinth His ambition's more important to him than what happens to us.

Victoria That's politicians all over.

Hyacinth I won't be long.

Hyacinth has another hug and exits

Maud She's a sharp-shins.

Maud exits with the tea trolley

Victoria I must go and get ready.

Victoria exits down the hall

Hyacinth returns with Jack Collingwood whom she met outside the front door. He carries binoculars and the "Sporting Life"

Hyacinth You look as though you're going to the races. Have you got something running, Uncle Jack?

Jack Have a bit each way on my horse in the three o'clock at Lingfield. It's called Passionate Lover.

Hyacinth Isn't that what they call you? I'll risk a quid at the betting shop round the corner. Should be OK with you as the owner and a name like that.

Jack Where are the others?

Hyacinth Julian's telling the magistrate he's an enemy of the working class. Mummy's dressing.

Jack And your father?

Hyacinth He's gone to fetch someone. (*She whispers*) I think it's his private secretary. There's some commotion about her.
Jack Yes, I heard.

The telephone rings, then stops

Hyacinth I believe Dad's keen on her.
Jack Not seriously I'm sure.
Hyacinth I'm off to the London Library. Good luck with your horse. Have you backed it?
Jack Certainly. It's time I won something off the Tote.

Hyacinth kisses Jack who holds on to her for rather too long for an avuncular good-bye kiss

Jack You're as attractive as your mother.
Hyacinth That's the best compliment I've had. (*Flustered*) Bye-bye, Uncle Jack. You do kiss nicely.

Hyacinth exits

Victoria enters, now wearing a summer dress and carrying her handbag

Victoria Jack. How wonderful to see you. I need you badly.
Jack Not as badly as I need you. (*He kisses her*)
Victoria I mean at this meeting.
Jack I'll be rooting for you. (*He tries to kiss her again*)
Victoria Stop. It's lovely but you're exciting me.
Jack I'm trying to.
Victoria You must think sometimes about something besides sex. This morning Philip has to be at the top of my thoughts—and they'll be here soon.

They sit down

Jack You weren't very friendly last night. I was frightened you'd stopped loving me already.
Victoria I didn't want to seem too intimate. I'm not used to sitting with a lover and a husband at the same time.
Jack Everything comes with practice.
Victoria And I was preoccupied with that cursed Miss Trafford.
Jack Romantics of Philip's age can be total idiots.
Victoria But not sophisticated predators like you.
Jack I do love you. Madly, particularly after yesterday.
Victoria But you wouldn't want to hurt Mary.
Jack I don't intend to.
Victoria Philip doesn't think of that. He behaves as if he were twenty.
Jack He's irresponsible.
Victoria Yet there's so much about him that's marvellous.

Philip and Jane are heard at the front door which he has opened with his key. They enter

Victoria and Jack separate

Victoria (*politely*) Good morning, Miss Trafford.
Philip Hallo, Jack.

Jack nods

Jane Good morning, Mrs Grantly.

They don't shake hands

Victoria Do you know Mr Collingwood?
Jane We've spoken on the telephone. Good morning, Mr Collingwood.
Jack Good morning, Miss Trafford, if you can call it good.

All laugh nervously

Victoria Well, it's begun with a little good news.
Philip (*eagerly*) What's that?
Victoria Mrs Brook-Green rang a moment ago. She says that the Science
Teacher analysed that stuff Hyacinth was snorting.
Philip Go on.
Victoria It was only Johnson's Baby Powder.
Jack She should change her dealer.
Philip Don't be facetious, Jack.
Victoria Mrs Brook-Green says they still take it very seriously but this time
they'll overlook it.
Philip I'm surprised Mrs Brook-Green has become so tolerant. I must have
shaken her over that Appeal Fund. Thank God that's out of the way.
Victoria Miss Trafford, perhaps you'd like to sit there. (*She points to the
sofa*) Here's a notepad for you to take the minutes.
Jane (*as she sits*) Won't Sir Edgar do that?
Victoria (*sweetly poisonous*) I thought you'd feel more at home with a
shorthand pad handy.
Jane I'm not that kind of secretary. I'm a top grade civil servant.
Victoria Sorry.
Philip He'll be here in a few minutes. Jack, how do you think we should
tackle it?
Jack (*awkwardly*) Well—er—it's a bit tricky. But Miss Trafford, I'm sure
you realize if sometime today the Prime Minister offers Mr Grantly, er, er
. . . Philip something, he can't possibly accept it.
Jane Under no circumstances?
Jack Not unless he knows the *News of the World* isn't going to print
anything about—um——
Jane Us having an affair? If we are having one.
Jack He couldn't let it blow up in the Prime Minister's face the very
moment an announcement is made. It would be dishonourable.
Jane I see. It would be more honourable to tell lies about it?
Jack You can't put it quite like that. On political matters it's honourable to
lie on behalf of the government.
Philip Governments can't exist if they always tell the truth.
Jack But it's dishonourable to lie about your sex life if you're bound to be
found out. Otherwise it's honourable. Have I made that clear?

Jane Perfectly. But I thought gentlemen always lied to protect a woman's reputation.

Jack You mustn't confuse politicians with gentlemen.

Jane Knowing Philip was encouraging me to make that mistake.

Philip Jane, you know I don't let people down.

Victoria You'll have to let someone down. We're not Muslims.

Jack The point is, Miss Trafford—I hope Philip won't mind me saying this—it's Philip's last chance. He's either onwards and upwards or downwards to oblivion.

Victoria Miss Trafford, would you want my husband if he were a nobody?

Jane Certainly. I love him for what he is, and not who he is.

Victoria You don't mind if he doesn't take you to the stars with him?

Jane (*sharply*) Did he tell you he said that?

Philip No!

Victoria (*sweetly*) He said it to me years ago. He'd be bound to use that line again and again. He's not very imaginative.

Jane (*dignified*) I mind deeply about Mr Grantly's career. If I have to, I'm prepared to do the honourable thing and tell lies. Then see how it works out later.

Victoria Miss Trafford, you mean I can have the temporary use of my husband on the understanding that you have the option to terminate my leasehold whenever it suits you? I'm not sure I find that an acceptable arrangement.

Philip But last night you were practically suggesting it.

Victoria What you feel late at night may not be the same as the morning after.

Philip Victoria's being unreasonable.

Jack Reasonable women are an affront to nature.

Philip She keeps changing her mind.

Jack Naturally.

Philip Why's Sir Edgar so late? It's eleven already.

Victoria It is Saturday morning.

Philip They'll have started printing their filthy smut if he's not here soon.

Jack Pull yourself together. You're going to pieces.

Philip I feel the whole world's in a conspiracy against me.

Jack Nonsense. You can rely on me for one.

Victoria (*smiling*) We all can. Good old reliable Jack.

The telephone rings. Victoria goes towards it

Philip Let me answer it. (*He seizes the telephone*) Philip Grantly here ... No I haven't heard anything, have you? ... Same to you. (*He puts the telephone down*) It was a terrified ex-minister who says his rich wife will leave him if he hasn't oiled his way back into the government.

Maud enters from the hall. She is carrying a large vase full of open roses. She goes to put them on a table

Maud I've changed the water. They looked jiggered like you all do this morning.

Victoria They're very pretty, Maud.

Jack Aren't they just?

Philip I remember now. There's something odd about how they got here . . .

The doorbell rings

Oh. (*Interrupting himself*) Thank God it's Sir Edgar at last.

As Maud starts going towards the front door

I'll let him in, Maud.

Philip exits

Maud goes down the hall

(*Off*) Good morning, Sir Edgar.

Philip enters with Sir Edgar, who carries a briefcase. He is business like and dressed in a City suit. He is authoritative, precise and neat, almost severe, but not inhuman

Sir Edgar (*as they enter*) Good morning, Mr Grantly.

Victoria Good morning, Sir Edgar.

Sir Edgar Good morning, Victoria.

Philip This is my Private Secretary, Miss Trafford.

Sir Edgar (*reflectively*) Ah, Miss Trafford. (*He shakes her hand*) How do you do?

Jane How do you do, Sir Edgar?

Philip I don't think you've met Jack Collingwood.

Sir Edgar Know him by name, of course. Ran the fifteen hundred metres in the Olympics before he ran into the obscurity of the House of Commons. How do you do?

Jack (*wincing*) I think I've heard that joke before, Sir Edgar. How do you do?

Philip Thank you, Sir Edgar, for coming at such short notice to cope with our sudden crisis. And on a Saturday morning.

Victoria It's very good of you.

Sir Edgar At your service, Madam. (*He bows in a courtly manner*) Urgency seems all important.

Philip I thought you might like to sit here and steer our craft through the rapids, Sir Edgar.

Sir Edgar moves to the breakfast table. He starts taking a large pad and some notes from his briefcase as the others except Philip begin to take their seats. Philip hesitates then sits

Sir Edgar How thoughtful. Now as I understand it the object of this meeting is to prevent the *News of the World* printing anything which might be—er—unhelpful to Mr Grantly. Are we all agreed on that?

Philip
Jack } (*together*) Yes, certainly. Absolutely
Jane

Sir Edgar Victoria?

Victoria It might be a relief to have a husband who was out of the vulgar scramble for power. If there's a scandal there'll be no point in his staying an MP.

Philip I wouldn't live in your pocket.

Victoria I could keep a closer eye on you. You know the Hungarian proverb, Sir Edgar?

Sir Edgar nods expectantly

"Opportunity makes the thief". There's too much opportunity for politicians.

Jane I believe Mr Grantly's career is of national importance.

Philip (*plaintively*) I thought you believed that, too, Victoria.

Victoria I've been reflecting on something Julian said. It doesn't matter which of you mediocrities are in the Cabinet. It only matters to the mediocrities.

Philip You can't take seriously the ranting of a political infant.

Victoria I wanted your success so you'd be happy, Philip. Like a golfer's wife who hates golf but wants him to win the Open. Why should I go on caring if it ends up making me unhappy?

Philip Because my career is the most important thing in this family. Objectively nothing else counts.

Sir Edgar Er—ahem—may we go on?

Victoria I'm sorry, Sir Edgar. I'm on edge this morning.

Sir Edgar Very natural in the circumstances. Before coming here, I took the precaution of ringing the Editor of the *News of the World* to find out what evidence they had of the allegations made yesterday evening. I said I was acting for Mr Grantly and that I would communicate with them later this morning. After I had consulted my client. (*He pauses to clear his throat*) I'm afraid this may be a trifle indelicate.

Jack Don't mind us.

Sir Edgar I meant for the ladies. It seems that the newspaper became aware of rumours that Mr Grantly and Miss Trafford were more friendly than is customary for a Minister and his Private Secretary. The Editor took the view that this was not in the public interest. Therefore the public should be acquainted with all the details.

Philip They pretend to support the government. They'd blow it up to sell a few more copies.

Sir Edgar It was not an appropriate moment to query the Editor's motives. (*He goes on*) Accordingly, a reporter, more than one reporter, were assigned to follow Mr Grantly and Miss Trafford.

Philip The nasty creeps.

Sir Edgar Among other places, they were observed together in a small London restaurant, of the type which has candles on the table, having dinner.

Philip There's nothing in that, Sir Edgar.

Sir Edgar It appears that sometimes they sat in close proximity—cheek by jowl as you might say. It is also suggested that they occasionally held each other's hands and er—Mr Grantly sometimes kissed Miss Trafford on the cheek and vice-versa.

Victoria M.T.F.

Sir Edgar What does that mean?

Victoria Must Touch Flesh. It's a disease. Philip's always suffered from it.

Philip Victoria!

Sir Edgar I see. Three nights ago they were followed from the retaurant to a block of flats in Chelsea. It is said that Miss Trafford let herself and Mr Grantly in with a key, and that Mr Grantly did not emerge for an hour and a quarter.

Philip Jane's flat-mate was in the flat while we were in the sitting room.

Sir Edgar Would she swear to it that nothing improper took place?

Jane I'm sure she would. She'd certainly say I would never make love on a sofa.

Jack laughs

Sir Edgar Excellent. Excellent. Then we come to yesterday. At about one o'clock Mr Grantly and Miss Trafford were observed entering this flat.

Victoria Oh, what a cheek!

Jack A bit risky, wasn't it Philip?

Philip (*to Jack*) Shut up.

Sir Edgar Can we avoid levity please? They were watched from the window of a second floor flat opposite, to which the porter had given access on the supposition that the journalist was a TV repair man. Unfortunately, or maybe fortunately, the owner of the flat returned. As she had not requested any repairs to her television set, the reporter made his excuses and left.

All save Sir Edgar laugh

Philip Usual dirty tricks.

Sir Edgar However, the reporter claims it was not before he had time to witness through his pocket telescope Mr Grantly and Miss Trafford in a warm embrace. He would go so far as to describe it as passionate. This is the basis for the *News of the World*'s allegation that Mr Grantly and Miss Trafford are having an affair. An allegation which they will print unless we can persuade them it would expose them to substantial damages for libel.

Maud enters carrying coffee cups etc on a tray

Maud I hope I'm not interrupting.

Victoria Would you like some coffee, Sir Edgar?

Sir Edgar That would be very welcome.

Victoria Could you take it round, Maud, please.

Maud starts taking the coffee round

Jane Sir Edgar, what is the definition of an affair?

Sir Edgar I should say it was an association in which—er—sexual intercourse was a regular feature.

Maud (*looking hard at Jane*) In this case I should say it were someone storming someone else's husband.

Sir Edgar Storming?

Maud Making him sloppy about her so she can pinch him. Excuse me blurting out what I think, but I've been with the family a long time.

Sir Edgar Not at all. What you say could well be an ingredient.

Maud exits

Victoria Don't worry about Maud, Sir Edgar. She's very discreet.

Sir Edgar Quite. Discretion is an essential attribute for a servant to someone in public life. Now, if I'm to be of any assistance I need to have the truth. Mr Grantly.

Philip It's, er, somewhat embarrassing. I'm not sure how to begin.

Jane I am. I trust you, Sir Edgar. I have made love with Mr Grantly once— and once only.

Sir Edgar May I ask when and where?

Jane Yesterday. (*Defiantly*) Here on the floor. Mr Grantly said Mrs Grantly wouldn't like it if we went into the bedroom.

Jack starts to laugh

Sir Edgar This is not a laughing matter.

Jack Sorry.

Sir Edgar And you can confirm that it was the only occasion, Miss Trafford?

Jane There hasn't been much chance since.

Sir Edgar If we are pressed on it, what would be the explanation for the warm embrace?

Jane A congratulatory hug. I'd just told Mr Grantly about my promotion from a Grade seven civil servant to a Grade five.

Sir Edgar As what, may I ask?

Jane As Assistant Secretary at the Home Office in charge of prisoners' moral welfare.

Philip I was delighted for her.

Sir Edgar But the, er, dinners and the er, um—hand-holding and kisses on the cheek?

Jane Mr Grantly has always taken a keen interest in my career as I have in his. We enjoy discussing our work.

Philip She looked on me as a father figure.

Victoria You're old enough to be her father.

Jane Maybe we've been over demonstrative but that doesn't prove we're having an affair.

Sir Edgar nods his agreement

Sir Edgar Quite.

Philip It was the sort of friendliness a man might share with a daughter.

Victoria Or a bimbo with a sugar daddy.

Jane That's insulting, Mrs Grantly.

Victoria It was meant to be, Miss Trafford. (*She turns to Sir Edgar*) Our defence is getting stronger, isn't it, Sir Edgar. You said an affair was an association in which sex was a regular feature. You can't say that once on my sitting room floor is that?

Jack I quite agree.

Victoria And you have no intention of doing it again, have you Miss Trafford?

Jane (*sulkily*) I suppose not. For the moment, anyway.

Sir Edgar I think I could brief Counsel that there has been nothing which amounts to what is generally understood by an "affair". And that Mr Grantly and Miss Trafford would strenuously deny it.

Philip Absolutely. It's an outrageous accusation against a man of my eminence.

Jane Of course.

Sir Edgar The *News of the World* can't prove anything. As to what is alleged about the restaurant and the—er—um—meeting here, I think we could get it dismissed as malicious and exaggerated tittle-tattle on which an untenable hypothesis has been built.

Philip Would a jury take my side on that?

Sir Edgar Juries find prurient Peeping Toms from the press reprehensible. Juries relish reading what the papers print but when they're in a jury box they assume a sanctimonious gravitas as good British citizens should. If they can, they mulct in heavy damages those who provide their secret amusement. The gentlemen of the press know that. That is their weakness. That is our strength.

Philip (*cheerfully*) What a relief. So we're pretty safe in warning off the *News of the World* without telling an outright lie?

Sir Edgar I should judge so. A jury might consider that you had sailed close to the limits of the circumspection expected of a minister. That is very different from sustaining the allegation of a continuing affair.

Philip When would a case come on?

Sir Edgar Not for around a year. If I speak to the Editor I very much doubt whether the *News of the World* will take the risk of printing anything. I take it we are all agreed that I should proceed along those lines?

Philip Certainly.

Jack Agreed.

Jane I'm willing that Sir Edgar handles it as he suggests.

Sir Edgar Victoria, you're saying nothing. But the ingenious proposal that a single—er——

Jack You mean a quickie?

Sir Edgar (*with distaste*) Thank you, Mr Collingwood. Very apt, I'm sure. (*He turns back to Victoria*) The proposal that a single event could not be classed as an affair in the accepted sense came from you, Victoria. I thought it worthy of a Queen's Counsel.

Victoria After your charming compliment, Sir Edgar, I agree that you should talk to the Editor of the *News of the World*.

Philip Thank you, Victoria. I knew you'd see a wife's momentarily injured feelings are not of national importance.

Victoria I shall reserve my final decision until I've heard how the Editor reacts.

Sir Edgar (*looking quizzically at Victoria*) Of course. We all have to do that. Now I would like to telephone the Editor of the *News of the World* to see if I can frighten them off. As I shall have to concentrate it would be as well to have no risk of interruption. Particularly, if I may say so without offence, from Mr Collingwood. Is there a telephone anywhere else that I could use?

Philip Of course, Sir Edgar. Along the hall. (*He points*) Last door on the right. There's one in the main bedroom.

Sir Edgar Thank you. I would be more comfortable in the bedroom.

Jack That's what I always say.

Sir Edgar exits down the passage giving Jack a look

Philip Shut up, Jack. You're making a pig of yourself.

Jack Calm down. You've got an even chance Sir Edgar may frighten them off.

Philip (*his eye lighting on the roses*) Those roses, Victoria. There's still something fishy about how they got here.

Jane (*now quite collected and slightly malicious*) I remember saying they must have come from an admirer. They were so lavish.

Victoria They came before I went out. From an admirer.

Philip Who?

Victoria That's my secret. And his. There was no card.

Philip Why didn't you tell the truth?

Victoria It's so unlike me to buy red roses that I never thought you'd believe me. I wanted to send you a hint you might have a rival.

Philip Damn silly.

Victoria And to stir your curiosity. Which it didn't till Miss Trafford prodded it.

Julian suddenly bursts in from the front door, looking excited. He carries his shoulder bag which he throws on a chair

Victoria Oh, Julian!

Julian Is this a secret meeting of Conservative dissidents?

Philip My God. I'd almost forgotten him. Miss Trafford, my son Julian.

They nod to each other

Julian Hallo, everyone.

They all nod

You all look very tragic.

Philip Never mind about us. What happened at Bow Street?

Julian Bound over to keep the peace for twelve months. The class biased Magistrate made a pompous speech about betraying my father.

Philip He's got his head screwed on.

Julian Only a capitalist court could pervert justice like that.

Philip Lucky you weren't in front of a Chinese communist court.
Julian You were right about one thing, Dad. The others had set me up. The
publicity was necessary in the interests of the struggle for working class
victory.
Philip Were there any reporters?
Julian (*complacently*) Dozens. I told them I was disgusted with the way the
Workers Revolutionary Party had used me. Said I was going to join the
Liberal Democrats.
Jack It could have been worse. It might have been the Greens.
Philip Some of those Labour fellows who joined the Lib-Democrats so
they'd be invited to smart parties will be delighted.
Julian They wouldn't be if they knew why, Dad. This is confidential. The
comrades decided I'm to infiltrate the Lib-Democrats under cover.
Jack Is that worth doing?
Julian Yes. The early Marxists began by developing very small cells. So my
next job is undermining that pathetic all-things-to-all-men lot.
Victoria Lovely, darling. Some of them are so good-looking. We'll ask them
to dinner. We'll give them your father's best claret.
Philip It removes any immediate damage to me. That's the main thing. Two
little ones down and the big one in the air.
Julian I'll leave you to your plotting.

As Sir Edgar enters

Good morning, Sir Edgar.
Sir Edgar Good morning. I thought plots were more your style.
Philip Buzz off, Julian.

The telephone rings. Julian goes for it

Philip Get out of my way, Julian.
Julian I'm expecting a call.
Philip So am I. However important you think your peculiar friends are they
don't rank above my life. (*He takes the telephone*) Philip Grantly speaking
... Hallo, George. No, nothing yet ... You're perfectly safe ... Thanks
for ringing. I'll let you know. (*He puts the telephone down*) That was a wet
Cabinet minister. I could do his job better than him. He thought he was
being engagingly frank when he said a touch of unemployment smartens
people up no end. (*He goes to sit down*) Sorry about that, Sir Edgar. How
did it go?

Julian exits down the hall, leaving his bag behind

Everyone looks expectantly at Sir Edgar, who sits down

Sir Edgar We got off to a bad start. The Editor claimed to have nothing but
goodwill towards you, Mr Grantly, regarding you as a personal friend.
Philip That ought to have helped.
Sir Edgar On the contrary. The Editor said knowing you so well, it was just
the sort of, and these were the words, silly ass sort of thing you would get

up to. That's why there was no doubt the story was true. And duty to the public came before friendship.

Philip Typical of hypocritical Fleet Street.

Sir Edgar Every profession, including politicians and lawyers, has its own hypocrisy. Without hypocrisy we would be shocking each other all the time. Hypocrisy is the cement of civilized conduct.

Jack So is money.

Sir Edgar Ah, you have gone to the nub of the matter, Mr Collingwood. I pointed out to the Editor that the evidence may seem inferential but it is not conclusive. That Mr Grantly and Miss Trafford were prepared to swear that they were not and have not been having an affair and that Mrs Grantly would firmly support them in this.

Philip I'm very grateful to you, Victoria.

Victoria is expressionless

Sir Edgar And that if any such allegation could be shown to have gravely affected Mr Grantly's prospects, the damages would be colossal.

Philip Then what happened?

Sir Edgar The Editor said they would drop the story.

Philip Thank God.

Jack That's a skinner for the book.

Jane Marvellous. Now you can accept anything decent the PM offers without worrying.

Philip Natural justice triumphed in the end. This calls for a drink.

Victoria Can we pause a moment? Now I've heard how Sir Edgar has temporarily silenced the *News of the World*——

All Temporarily!

Sir Edgar I was half expecting a last minute hitch.

Victoria Sir Edgar, though my husband has technically not had an affair, he has committed adultery, hasn't he?

Sir Edgar That is an inescapable fact.

Victoria And nothing I have said or done so far amounts to my condoning it?

Sir Edgar That is also true.

Victoria So if I tell the *News of the World* this morning that I intend to sue my husband for divorce citing Miss Trafford as co-respondent . . .

Jane It would destroy his life!

Jack It would finish him politically!

Philip You couldn't do such a rotten thing.

Victoria It's what I'm going to do.

Jack That's not the sense of this meeting, Victoria.

Philip Hear, hear! You tell her, Jack.

Sir Edgar smiles and Jane looks apprehensive

Victoria But I won't on one condition. That Miss Trafford and my husband solemnly promise here and now that neither of them will seek to break up my marriage.

Philip That's an abominable use of power gained by despicable snooping, Victoria.

Victoria It would be a renewal of our marriage vows. For better or for worse. I always liked that passage.

Jane You can't police people's emotions, Mrs Grantly.

Victoria It's not your emotions I'm interested in. It's your behaviour.

Jane This is awful. (*She starts crying and reaches for Philip's hand*)

Victoria Stop trying to get your way by playing the injured little girl. Remember that you've just been appointed to look after the moral welfare of Her Majesty's guests.

Jane (*taking her hand away, sitting up and stopping crying*) You are as cruel as Medusa, Mrs Grantly. Though perhaps not quite as ugly.

Victoria Vitriol from ancient Greece won't help my husband. His only hope is for me to stay my hand.

Philip That's blackmail.

Victoria It's Miss Trafford's chance for moral glory. His divine right to fulfill himself. His country needs him. That's what you really care about, isn't it Miss Trafford?

Philip You're making a mock of what drew me to politics, Victoria. My dedication to helping everyone have a better life. Particularly those at the bottom of the heap.

Victoria Miss Trafford's renunciation in so noble a cause would be the quintessence of romance, like a Brontë novel.

Sir Edgar It wouldn't be legally binding.

Victoria I've thought of that. In case my husband succumbs to Miss Trafford's wiles later, I want a settlement. If there were ever a divorce or separation—and whoever might be the so-called guilty party—

Jack holds up his hand to his face

—I want an undertaking that all Philip's property should become mine. Would that be legally binding, Sir Edgar?

Philip It's blatant blackmail.

Sir Edgar In layman's terms it may be blackmail. But if two spouses are at breaking point and on the verge of separating for good—and there's not much doubt about that here—they can come to a legal agreement on any terms they choose for cohabitation not to end but to continue. That would be valid and binding.

Philip Does that mean Victoria could behave as badly as she pleased and I can't?

Sir Edgar That would be her privilege. I don't think you could attack such an agreement even if Victoria had—er—had strayed before it was made. Or afterwards. (*Hastily*) Though I'm sure there's no likelihood of that.

Jack Of course not.

Philip That's bloody unfair.

Sir Edgar You don't have to make the agreement, Mr Grantly, if you don't want to.

Philip But if I married Jane it would mean I'd have to leave politics. We'd have nothing decent to live on after Victoria had swiped the lot— including my holdings in Grantly & Keswick.

Victoria (*triumphant again*) Ah, true love, dear, soars above money. And you could always look forward to living on Miss Trafford's ever growing index-linked pension.

Philip I know it's my fault we're in this dreadful mess, Jane.

Jane It's fiendish. I love you too much to ruin your career. I promise not to break up your marriage. (*Hopefully*) Perhaps Philip won't feel the same?

Philip (*hesitating and ashamed*) I've let you down, Jane. It's unforgivable after what we've meant to each other. But I'd be a wretched companion if I was out of politics. It's my whole life. Victoria, you win. It's horrible, Jane, but there are some things——

Victoria Which are bigger than both of you?

Philip Don't rub it in, Victoria. I've agreed.

Jane The cards are stacked against me. I have no option.

Victoria The family's intact. And my foolish husband is still mine. In spite of his straying I wouldn't want a different one.

Philip goes over to Victoria. The telephone rings

Could you answer that please, Jack.

Julian enters

Jack goes to the telephone

Julian I'm expecting an important call. (*He moves towards the telephone*)

Philip I'm expecting a call which could be even more important than yours, Julian, if that were possible. I'll answer it. (*He does*)

Julian picks up his bag

Philip (*on the phone*) Hallo . . . It is. The Prime Minister wants to speak to me. Be quiet everyone. Hallo, Prime Minister . . . Just quietly thinking out a few suggestions for your next ten years.

Julian drops the bag with a thud

I should be honoured to accept . . . It's what I've always wanted to do. Thank you for your confidence in me . . . Yes. I'll be in my new office on Monday . . . Victoria's fine . . . I'm sure she'll be delighted. Thank you so much, Prime Minister. You can count on my loyalty. (*He puts down the telephone and walks deliberately but not elatedly to sit slowly*)

Victoria, Jane, Jack and Julian are standing

All (*variously*) What is it, Philip? (*Or Dad*)

Philip (*gloomily*) I'm to be Chancellor——

Jack Chancellor!

Philip —of the Duchy of Lancaster. I get a seat in the Cabinet.

All Congratulations.

Philip I shall have special responsibility for devising a healthy diet for the nation, particularly school children.

Victoria You've always been keen on that.

Philip And for introducing legislation so that people can know whether what they're eating is good or bad for them.

Sir Edgar If I may say so, you're admirably fitted to the task. Devoting your undoubted abilities to the subject should bring great benefits to the health of the country.

Philip Thank you, Sir Edgar. (*Sadly*) But part of the deal is that I've got to go to the House of Lords.

Victoria Hooray! No more frightful constituents. I shall be Lady Grantly. And Philip will have to buy me a diamond tiara for the State Opening of Parliament.

Julian You're such a second rate snob, Ma.

Victoria Without the great army of the second rate there'd be nothing for the first rate to shine against.

Jack Look out, you'll be the Honourable Julian Grantly.

Julian I shan't use any bloody title.

Jack You'll have to in the Liberal Democrats. Or your cover will be blown.

Philip None of you understand. Now I'm in the Lords I can never be Prime Minister. Lord Grantly of Lower Slaughter would be an appropriate choice for my title.

Sir Edgar Don't despair, my dear fellow.

Philip I suppose it was always an empty dream that I might be Prime Minister. But it hurts when a dream disappears.

Jack You'll be much nearer the top in politics. If you can't be king you can be a kingmaker.

Philip (*brightening*) There is that. I could be like Willie Whitelaw when he went to the Lords.

Jack He was the second most important person in the country.

Philip And there could be a special law to let me renounce my peerage and go back to the Commons as PM just as dear old Alec Douglas Home did.

Sir Edgar Good luck, Lord Grantly and don't feel guilty about your private behaviour. It's been no different from the people you represent. It's just that any—er—little human *contretemps* politicians may be mixed up in is magnified a hundred fold if it catches the public glare. Something to keep out of in future I suggest.

Philip Victoria will see to that.

Victoria goes up to a pleased but embarrassed Sir Edgar, throws her arms around him and kisses his forehead

Victoria Sir Edgar, you're adorable.

Philip Thank you for everything, Sir Edgar.

Sir Edgar Not at all. I'm glad we're still upright after the roaring rapids.

Victoria opens her bag. She takes out a large diamond bracelet

Victoria Philip, can you help me put this on?

Philip I haven't seen that before. How pretty.

Victoria I'm glad you like it.

Philip When did you get it?

Victoria On my way to Wimbledon yesterday.

Jack It's gorgeous.

Philip It must have been a jolly good shop. The diamonds look almost real.

Victoria They are. *Cartier*. Remember?

Philip My God, *Cartier* of course! Was it a present from rich Aunt Anne?

Victoria No.

Philip Who gave it you then?

Victoria You did.

Philip I did! How much did it cost?

Victoria Forty three thousand pounds.

Philip Crikey!

Julian Filthy capitalist ostentation.

Victoria Here's the bill. (*She takes it out of her bag and gives it to him*)

Jack I'm glad that's not my bill.

Victoria I'd never compromise myself by giving you a bill, Jack.

Philip It's preposterous.

Jack No, it's the wages of sin. You're lucky to have bought a peerage and a seat in the Cabinet so cheaply.

Philip It's cost me more than money.

Victoria A good wife is beyond price.

Jane Mistresses have their price, too.

Victoria How vulgar.

Jane It's you who are vulgar. It isn't money I meant. That's your preoccupation.

Victoria What do you mean?

Jane Perhaps Philip's beginning to understand.

Philip No, not altogether.

Sir Edgar I believe I do, Miss Trafford. The true price of a mistress is you never know how much havoc she can wreak. Or when.

Jane I thought you might guess, Sir Edgar. Who do you think had the *News of the World* tipped off in the first place. I thought it would force his Lordship into being honourable enough to marry me. Goodbye everyone.

Jane turns to go. Philip sinks on to a chair and everyone looks astonished

CURTAIN

FURNITURE AND PROPERTY LIST

ACT 1

SCENE 1

No props required

SCENE 2

The Westminster flat

On stage: Sofa
Rug
Armchairs
Occasional tables
Lamps
Dining table and four chairs
Small side-board. *On it:* hotplate
Cupboard. *In it:* bottles, glasses, small fridge
Wastepaper basket
Pictures
Vases

Off stage: Trolley. *On it:* breakfast things **(Maud)**
Red dispatch case **(Philip)**
Copy of the Daily Telegraph **(Philip)**
Butter **(Maud)**
Coffee cup **(Victoria)**
Philip's dinner jacket. *In a pocket:* pen and a piece of paper **(Victoria)**
Satchel. *In it:* a couple of books and some home-made cigarettes **(Hyacinth)**
Large, bulging cloth bag **(Maud)**

Personal: **Philip:** wallet. *In it:* two ten pound notes
Philip: watch (worn throughout)

SCENE 3

No props required

SCENE 4

The Westminster flat

Set: Jug of water in cupboard

Off stage: Huge bunch of red roses **(Jack)**
Handbag. *In it:* piece of paper **(Victoria)**

SCENE 5

Personal: **Philip:** dispatch box

SCENE 6

The Westminster flat

Set: Three half-bottles of champagne in the fridge

Off stage: Dispatch box. *In it:* three sandwiches wrapped in a napkin **(Philip)**

Personal: **Jane:** diamond bracelet

SCENE 7

On stage: As before

Off stage: Dispatch box **(Philip)**
             Bag of books **(Hyacinth)**
             Chicken leg **(Hyacinth)**

ACT II

SCENE 1 (Inset scene)

On stage: Two chairs

Personal: **Philip:** balloon glass of brandy

SCENE 2

The Westminster flat

Off stage: Cup of coffee **(Maud)**

Personal: **Victoria:** handbag. *In it:* note

SCENE 3 (Inset scene)

On stage: Two armchairs

Off stage: Bottle of champagne and two silver mugs **(Jack** and **Philip)**

SCENE 4

The Westminster flat

Strike: Roses

Set: Used breakfast things on the trolley

Off stage: Notepad **(Victoria)**
             Empty book bag **(Hyacinth)**
             Binoculars, copy of *The Sporting Life* **(Jack)**
             Handbag. *In it:* bill and diamond bracelet **(Victoria)**
             Large vase of open roses **(Maud)**

Tray. *On it:* coffee cups **(Maud)**
Shoulder bag **(Julian)**

Personal: **Maud:** Duster and polish

LIGHTING PLOT

Property fittings required: nil

2 interior settings

ACT I, SCENE 1

To open: Spotlight on **Philip**

Cue 1   **Philip:** "... nothing could go wrong."   (Page 1)
         Black-out

ACT I, SCENE 2

To open: Bright sunshine

Cue 2   **Victoria:** "She's got the bracelet already."   (Page 11)
         Lights cross-fade to **Philip**

ACT 1, SCENE 3

To open: Spotlight on **Philip**

Cue 3   **Philip:** "I don't let him dominate me."   (Page 11)
         Lights cross-fade to the sitting-room

ACT 1, SCENE 4

To open: Full general lighting

Cue 4   **Victoria** and **Jack** ease down to the rug   (Page 16)
         Fade to Black-out

ACT 1, SCENE 5

To open: Spotlight on **Philip**

Cue 5   **Philip:** "... might just take the heat off me."   (Page 17)
         Lights cross-fade to sitting-room

ACT 1, SCENE 6

To open: Full general lighting

Cue 6   **Philip:** "I've a high profile ..."   (Page 20)
         Room darkens slightly

Cue 7   **Philip** eases her on to the rug   (Page 21)
         Black-out

ACT 1, SCENE 7.   Early evening

To open: Cloudy dusk

No cues

ACT 2, SCENE 1.   Evening

To open: Overall general lighting

Cue 8   **Philip** and **Victoria** exit   (Page 30)
           Lights fade

ACT 2, SCENE 2.   Night

To open: Darkness

Cue 9   **Julian** turns on the lights   (Page 30)
           Snap on full general lighting

Cue 10   **Victoria** goes to the telephone   (Page 38)
           Lights cross-fade to the Garrick Club

ACT 2, SCENE 3.   Night

To open: Overall general lighting

Cue 11   **Jack** exits   (Page 40)
           Lights cross-fade to the sitting room

ACT 2, SCENE 4.   Morning

To open: Full general lighting

No Cues

EFFECTS PLOT

ACT I

Cue 1	**Maud** enters *Telephone rings*	(Page 2)
Cue 2	**Victoria** picks up the telephone *Telephone stops ringing*	(Page 2)
Cue 3	**Victoria** goes to the telephone *Telephone rings*	(Page 10)
Cue 4	**Victoria** picks up the telephone *Telephone stops ringing*	(Page 10)
Cue 5	To open scene 4 *The doorbell rings several times*	(Page 11)
Cue 6	**Philip** eases her on to the rug *Thunder and lightning*	(Page 21)
Cue 7	**Victoria** straightens the rug *Telephone rings*	(Page 21)
Cue 8	**Victoria** answers the telephone *Telephone stops ringing*	(Page 21)
Cue 9	**Hyacinth:** ". . . not knowing the score." *Telephone rings*	(Page 27)
Cue 10	**Victoria** answers the telephone *Telephone stops ringing*	(Page 27)
Cue 11	**Victoria:** ". . . Telecom was privatised." *Telephone rings*	(Page 27)
Cue 12	**Victoria** answers it *Telephone stops*	(Page 27)
Cue 13	**Philip:** ". . . won't be very late." *Telephone rings*	(Page 27)
Cue 14	**Philip** picks up the telephone *Telephone stops ringing*	(Page 27)
Cue 15	**Hyacinth** exits *Telephone rings*	(Page 27)
Cue 16	**Hyacinth** answers the telephone *Telephone stops ringing*	(Page 27)
Cue 17	**Hyacinth** puts the telephone down *Telephone rings*	(Page 28)

Cue 18   **Hyacinth** answers the telephone   (Page 28)
         Telephone stops ringing

ACT II

Cue 19   **Victoria:** "Lovely."   (Page 32)
         Telephone rings

Cue 20   **Philip** picks up the telephone   (Page 32)
         Telephone stops ringing

Cue 21   **Julian** and **Hyacinth** exit   (Page 33)
         Telephone rings

Cue 22   **Victoria** answers it   (Page 33)
         Telephone stops ringing

Cue 23   **Jack:** "Yes, I heard."   (Page 42)
         Telephone rings then stops

Cue 24   **Victoria:** "Good old reliable Jack."   (Page 44)
         Telephone rings

Cue 25   **Philip** answers the telephone   (Page 44)
         Telephone stops ringing

Cue 26   **Philip:** "... they got here ..."   (Page 45)
         Doorbell rings

Cue 27   **Philip:** "Buzz off, Julian."   (Page 51)
         Telephone rings

Cue 28   **Philip** answers the telephone   (Page 51)
         Telephone stops ringing

Cue 29   **Philip** goes over to Victoria   (Page 54)
         Telephone rings

Cue 30   **Philip** answers the telephone   (Page 54)
         Telephone stops ringing